Women
and the
Enlightenment

The *Women & History* series:

Women
and the
Enlightenment

Margaret Hunt, Margaret Jacob,
Phyllis Mack, and Ruth Perry

Copublished by
The Institute for Research in History and The Haworth Press, Inc.

Women and the Enlightenment has also been published as *Women & History*, Number 9, Spring 1984.

The Haworth Press, Inc., 10 Alice Street, Binghamton, NY 13904–1580

Library of Congress Cataloging in Publication Data
Main entry under title:

Women and the Enlightenment.

Also published as Women & history, no. 9, Spring 1984.

Includes bibliographical references and index.
1. Women—Europe—History—Addresses, essays, lectures. 2. Enlightenment—Addresses, essays, lectures. 3. Astell, Mary, 1666-1731—Addresses, essays, lectures. 4. Women in the book industries and trade—England—London—History—Addresses, essays, lectures. 5. Women and freemasonry—Netherlands—Hague—History—Addresses, essays, lectures. I. Hunt, Margaret. II. Institute for Research in History (New York, N.Y.)
HQ1587.W65   1984   305.4'094   84-590
ISBN 0-86656-190-0

In Memory of Joan Kelly

Women and the Enlightenment

Women & History
Number 9

CONTENTS

Foreword

Was there an Enlightenment for women? Yes, if the Enlightenment is seen not simply as the preserve of a narrow segment of intellectuals, but as a new way of perceiving and living one's life by ordinary people—artisans, women, and others—who were often far removed from the *philosophes*. As the essays in this volume make clear, women's responses to the Enlightenment should be understood in different terms from their 'high culture' male contemporaries.

Ruth Perry writes of the celebrated Mary Astell who, though usually not considered among the English enlightened philosophers, nonetheless joined the disputes of Locke, Shaftsbury, and their contemporaries, and surprised them all by being a woman who used right reason to refute their arguments. As a conservative Tory, her relation to the Enlightenment was complex. She defended the Church of England against the "progressive" values of the English deists, and upheld the traditional Stuart monarchy against the newfangled belief in more democratic representation. As a 'spinister' in a society which had little use for unmarried women, she insisted on women's intellectual equality and advocated education for all women. This intellectual woman with her counter-Enlightenment attitudes was a manifestation of the spirit of the times she so resisted.

The remarkable women in Margaret Hunt's essay plied their publishing trades in London in defiance of the authorities. Many of them risked prison by daring to circulate tracts which challenged the tenets of the Whig oligarchy's Church of England. The proliferation of the printed word in England, made possible by the increase of literacy and the growth of commerce, was unmatched on the continent. These women were part of the exciting new world of printing. But they were not merely good businesswomen; the London hawkers and mercuries had a stake in the Enlightenment. The cohesion of their families—of mothers and daughters, in particular—abetted their survival in an unequal struggle with the law.

Margaret Jacob's essay describes an unusual lodge of freemasons in the Hague which admitted women, despite the prohibition of the masonic constitutions that "no bondsman, no women, no immoral and scandalous men" may belong to any lodge. As members of this lodge, women took oaths of secrecy and subscribed to the pantheism of the radical Enlightenment. Many of these women were actresses and managers of the Comédie Française, housed in the Hague. Although in France actresses who had at their command an amazing repertoire of the classical French theatre, were considered immoral by the Church, this prejudice did not debar them from the more democratic lodge in the Hague. Margaret Jacob suggests that the exclusivity of freemasonry, protected by secrecy, permitted the women in this particular lodge to share in the Enlightenment.

In her Introduction Phyllis Mack explores the themes of the three essays and comments on the intellectual and material transformations brought about by the scientific revolution and how these transformations affected the world of women. Despite their differing responses to the Enlightenment, the women in all three essays claimed a more vocal participation in the arena of controversy than would have been possible in an earlier age.

We must try to understand how eighteenth-century women understood themselves and their needs, and not as contemporary men perceived them, nor as we in the twentieth century perceive them. We must reread these women authors of the eighteenth century to discover what the Enlightenment meant to them. We must broaden our concept of the Enlightenment by discovering women as yet unheard of. We shall continue to search, for, as another male figure of the Enlightenment once wrote, we must cultivate our *own* garden.

Ruth Graham
The Institute for Research in History

Women
and the
Enlightenment

Women and the Enlightenment: Introduction

Phyllis Mack

The period of European history from the mid-seventeenth to the mid-eighteenth century was dominated by extraordinary events: political and economic upheavals, religious conflict and consolidation, and the intellectual transformation known as the scientific revolution. The essays in this volume explore the impact of these social and intellectual transformations on the world of women. What was the content and function of women's public life during the period of political and economic chaos, and how did both content and function change during a period of political consolidation and economic expansion? How did the development of scientific thought—the replacement of a religious cosmology by a world view that was materialist and secular—affect perceptions about the attributes of gender? And how did the symbols and stereotypes of Womanhood expressed by men—doctors, philosophers, politicians, prophets—affect the self-images and behavior of thoughtful women? Did European women experience an Enlightenment?

During the seventeenth century, most men and women sustained their faith in the importance of religious values, if not the validity of particular religious traditions. They also believed that, were the universe ever completely understood, it would reveal itself to be a single, harmonious totality. Their physical and social world was not compartmentalized but full of analogies, so that the movements of the planets, the structure and functions of government and society, and the private realms of emotional life and personal physiology were all linked together in a single cosmic design. Political thinkers wrote about the state as a macrocosm of the family, with the king as father and husband, parliament as the wife, and the populace as obedient children. "It is true indeed," the prophet

Phyllis Mack teaches at Rutgers University and is Acting Director of the Rutgers Institute for Research on Women.

1

Elizabeth Poole declared to an audience of parliamentary soldiers
during the English revolution.

> . . . the king is your father and husband, which you were and
> are to obey in the Lord, and in no other way, for when he
> forgot his subordination to divine faithhood and headship,
> thinking he had begotten you a generation to his own plea-
> sure, and taking you a wife for his own lusts, thereby is the
> yoke taken from your necks.[1]

These supposed affinities between public and private, and between nature and spirit, also affected perceptions about the attributes of gender. Because a woman menstruated, her nature was
viewed as similar to that of the moon and tides, which shared her
monthly cycle. And since the moon shone only with the cold, reflected light of the sun, so women were by nature cold, moist and
passive. They could also be sinister; just as the moon was linked to
night and mystery, so women had a special affinity with the forces
of malevolence that lived in darkness; this formed part of the ra-
tionale for the predominance of women among those accused of
witchcraft. Men, on the other hand, were thought to be like the
sun, which radiates life-giving energy. Men belonged to the world
of daylight. They were clear-headed, rational, hot and dry. In the
seventeenth century babies were washed in salt water at birth to
dry out their brains and strengthen their wit.[2]
   The main impact of all this symbolic baggage on the lives of actual women was certainly negative. Women were thought to be unfit for public citizenship or positions of intellectual eminence; and
in fact there was no self-conscious, clear-cut women's politics in
the early modern period. But outside the natural political order, in
the sphere of spirituality or religious culture—there women *could*
be accepted as figures of authority. "Nature hath put a firceness
into the female," wrote a Puritan pastor.

> . . . therefore the she-bear and the lyoness are the most rag-
> ing and cruel. But grace makes that naturall impotency of the
> woman, turne impotency for God. Their nature, being fear-
> ful, hath ever been proner to superstition. Men's spirits are
> hardier, do not so easily fear Majesty, tremble at judgements,
> beleeve promises, shun sin, love God as women; so that
> when they are in the way, none are better.[3]

And so when women *did* enter the public arena, it was in their cultural capacity as symbolic figures or—when they participated in popular disturbances—as vessels of God's word or vengeance. Women were visible during the seventeenth century not only as witches, but also as visionaries who were prominent in social and political movements. Their own writings reflected popular conceptions of femininity as both holy and demonic, but they also used feminine themes creatively, as in the prophet Mary Cary's vision of an apocalypse of healthy children, or the visionary Jane Lead's use of biblical figures as metaphors to comment on the condition of marriage and widowhood.[4]

The symbolic weight of a woman in public was nowhere better understood or exploited than by Elizabeth I, who sustained national unity around the persona of Astraea, the Virgin Empress.[5] For even queens did not leave the domestic, female, spiritual world to act as rational public citizens. On the contrary; it was in their capacity as women—irrational, emotional, permeable, and therefore susceptible to invasion by spiritual forces,—that women were tolerated as preachers, missionaries and public speakers. And it was in their capacity as household members that they worked, carrying on the domestic occupations of medicine, brewing, manufacturing textiles, farming, or midwifery.[6]

* * *

Eighteenth century writers on science and society demolished most of these ideas about humanity and its relation to the natural order. The philosophes wrote of human nature as a universal category, and of human behavior as susceptible of scientific investigation; that is, conforming to forces of self-interest or environmental influence which paralleled those of motion and gravity in the physical universe. But how did all of this affect their ideas about women? Once the occult affinities between the attributes of the cosmos and those of gender were no longer intellectually credible, what was the effect on perceptions about the nature of Woman and on the self-images of thoughtful women themselves?

We know, for one thing, that the persecution of women as witches was slowly abandoned; in fact both the witch and the prophet came to be viewed with compassion or ridicule as medical phenomena or social rejects.[7] But popular notions about women's dual nature were remarkably resilient during the eighteenth century, even without the buttress of the conception of nature as both benevolent and sinister. Ministers, political theorists and doctors still described women as emotional, passive and permeable, and they still linked women both to the life-giving forces of nature as instruments of moral regeneration (as in the notion of romantic motherhood) and to the forces of anarchy and disorder (as, for example, in the image of Credit-finance as a woman).[8] Certainly the polarities of the virgin/witch myth became less stark, but the ambiguity about the female nature was no less intense, and it was buttressed even more firmly by a physiology which stressed the reciprocal effect of mind and body—women's bodies having a greater sway over their minds than men's.[9]

Given the profound changes in theory and attitude about both humanity and the physical universe during the Enlightenment, why were attitudes about the female nature so persistent? One reason was surely the altered political and religious climate of eighteenth century Europe. During the seventeenth century, feminine symbols and stereotypes had often been linked to myths about the oppressed in general; they served as a catalyst for political opposition and as a justification for political action. Radicals of various sorts and classes spoke of the oppressed and of women in the same breath as the true servants of God; they used the discourse on women as an instrument of challenge as well as an instrument of victimization, to borrow the terminology of Michel Foucault.[10] (Although to be sure, the challenge was not on behalf of women. If mystics, Puritans and sectarians were identified with Woman as loving and pious, the forces of evil—the aristocracy or the clergy—were also identified with Woman, now defined as greedy, lustful and vain). As social and political categories became more fluid, so did the categories of gender: Thus Puritan ministers referred to themselves as the breasts of God, mystical writers—both male and female—used metaphors of maternal love to describe their visionary experience, and Quaker prophets, in an effort to express the ecstasy of their reborn condition, actually switched sexes; women announced that they were now men, and men identified themselves, metaphorically at least, as women.[11]

But the political understanding of mystics and religious radicals who evoked the image of the Whore of Babylon was very different from that of the eighteenth century writers who depicted Credit as a passionate woman. The eighteenth century discourse on women functioned not as an instrument of challenge, but as a device to impose order on a society in which change was perceived to be at once desirable and threatening. Many writers continued to acknowledge the passion and energy symbolized by Woman as a positive force, but their impulse to control that force was much more urgent than before because of their anxiety to avoid the horrors of religious violence, which they associated with unrestrained, feminine enthusiasm. Jonathan Swift, for one, linked enthusiasm in its most execrable forms with women; he took particular aim at "Female Priests" or "Quakers who suffer their Women to preach and pray," comparing them to ancient oracular priestesses:

> It is true indeed, that these (oracles) were frequently managed and directed by Female Officers, whose Organs were understood to be better disposed for the Admission of those Oracular Gusts, as entering and passing up thro' a Receptacle of greater Capacity, and causing also a Pruriency by the Way, such as with due Management, hath been refined from a Carnal, into a Spiritual Extasie.[12]

How clever of Swift to satirize religious ecstasy while reinforcing prejudices about women's propensity for carnality and invasion by occult forces! By linking religious fanaticism to femininity, Enlightenment thinkers could feel absolved from blame for past excesses and be assured that the seeds of fanaticism would not germinate in the breasts of upstanding male citizens.

The rejection of passionate enthusiasm as neither a socially acceptable nor a spiritually valid mode of behavior is striking in the internal development of English Quakerism during this period, when, because of their desire to become respectable citizens, men and women colluded in the muzzling of prophetic writers and in the restriction of women preachers to a more restrained, less public role within the Quaker community. Working class radicals apparently felt less compunction to avoid identifying with visionary women. The eighteenth century heirs of early Quaker radicalism, and of the early Quakers' emphasis on feminine symbolism and female public leadership, were the Shakers; a movement explicitly and narrowly created by Ann Lee in the interests of the laboring class.[13]

Certainly the anti-clericalism and satirical tone of Enlightenment literature sound more 'progressive' to the modern ear than the visionary writing of earlier periods, as do the pleas in many eighteenth century journals for the education of women. To these writers, the term "human being" ostensibly meant one whose development had not been distorted by religious education or corrupt aristocratic taste; but it also meant one whose personality was not distorted by enthusiasm or undue emotion. So in fact, the enlightened view of what constituted virtue may have become less flexible during the eighteenth century, when the ideal, fully developed human being became defined by restraint, rationality, and orientation toward socially useful goals. Such a person was unquestionably male and in the middling or higher ranks of society. According to one modern observer.

> The ideology of progress which was so deeply entrenched in Enlightenment thought meant that the growth of a humane, rational and civilized society could also be seen as a struggle between the sexes, with men imposing their value systems on women in order to facilitate social progress. Human history, the growth of culture through the domination of nature, was the increasing assertion of masculine ways over irrational, backward-looking women.[14]

Indeed, for many intellectuals, the categories of gender became almost completely polarized during the Enlightenment; thus medical men wrote about masculine Science penetrating passive, feminine Nature, political theorists advocated a style of public thought and action based on reason divorced from passion, and religious thinkers rejected enthusiasm in favor of a "strong, steady, masculine Piety," as Joseph Addison put it in an issue of *The Spectator*.[15] Margaret Jacob offers fascinating evidence of this hardening of attitudes about issues relating to gender in her description of homophobic riots in the Netherlands during 1730-31.[16]

My hypothesis is that the experience of women during the Enlightenment may have been similar to that of European Jews, whose social emancipation was conditional on their ability to assimilate, or to strip themselves of their ethnicity—those peculiarities of tradition and behavior that made them Jewish. Many contemporary Jews portrayed themselves as eager to dispense with the anachronisms of their cultural heritage, which they saw as the unfortunate result of a deprived environment (and which, incidentally, included supposed personal characteristics, such as heightened sexual appetite and the propensity toward religious fanaticism, which were also associated with women). 'We may look different from you Christians,' progressive Jews seemed to be saying, 'but we're all gentlemen under the skin.'

Middle class women also gained a degree of intellectual emancipation during the Enlightenment—an eighteenth century educated woman might actually earn her own living through writing or journalism. Women produced the majority of all novels published in England in the second half of the century; women also constituted, for the first time in European history, a large segment of the reading public.[17] Given prevalent attitudes toward enthusiasm and the propensity of women to impulsive behavior, some of these enlightened women may have believed, as their Jewish contemporaries did, that their social and intellectual emancipation was conditional on their ability to divest themselves of 'deviant' feminine character traits. This seems to have been the unconscious attitude of at least one important Enlightenment figure—the writer Mary Astell.

Ruth Perry sees the core of Astell's modernity in her perception of the Self as rational intellect, utterly detached from the passions and appetites. "The appetites," writes Perry, "had a different purpose . . . they were to preserve the body. They could not be trusted to assess the spiritual meaning of experience; steady Reason was the only proper instrument for determining Truth.[18] She also describes Astell's vision of celibate female collectivities; colleges for elite women who were already intellectually developed and who were also, one suspects, already somewhat detached from the artificial, feminine qualities of vanity, pettiness and greed —artificial, because they are induced by women's limited social environment.

At first glance, Astell's rather austere vision seems like an updated version of the convent as well as a reflection of personal psychology. I think that, consciously or not, Astell may have also anticipated the Enlightenment notion of what it was to be truly civilized. It is as if she could only conceive of feminine emancipation by eliminating feminine attributes; just as Eastern European Jews had to shave off their sidelocks and think like Establishment Christians in order to be accepted as full members of the human race, so women would have to leave off their ornaments, frivolities and emotions and think like rational men. Astell's ideas are particularly interesting compared to those of Lady Anne Conway, a seventeenth century writer who, like Astell, corresponded with contemporary Platonic thinkers but who, unlike Astell, embraced the idea of the Self or Soul as partly intuitive, and who ultimately became a Quaker and a proponent of the quasi-mystical doctrine of the Inner Light.[19]

In any case, Mary Astell's Enlightenment was a secret one, restricted to the secluded world of the home or female college. In her study of Freemasonry in the Hague, Margaret Jacob observes that European women experienced absolute equality with men only in the secret confines of certain masonic lodges. She further suggests that the theatrical imagination of the actresses who joined the lodge was what enabled them to invent and practice their egalitarian rituals. It might also have convinced the male middle and upper class members, many of whom were not actors, that the women were somehow unreal, being neither salonières nor members of conventional households. As Jacob observes, the rituals of the lodge appealed to the male members as a kind of Enlightenment fantasy, similar to the contemporary literature set in Tahiti or El Dorado that was so popular, so sexually and politically titillating and, because of its exoticism, so fundamentally harmless.

Whatever the ambiguities of women's social and intellectual status during the Enlightenment, opportunities for some working women apparently increased. All three essays suggest that as class differences became more pronounced during this period of developing capitalism, it was plebian and working women, not salonières, who experienced an Enlightenment, if we accept Peter Gay's definition of Enlightenment as achieving some kind of adult, personal autonomy. Perry sees Mary Astell as an Enlightenment figure less because of her ideas than because she worked as a professional writer. In this sense she was a precursor of the bluestockings of the later eighteenth century, who flourished as writers, translators, farmers and heads of households as well as conversationalists.[20] Margaret Hunt links the large number of women in the English publishing trades to the rapid expansion in the distribution of printed matter during the early years of the century. She demonstrates the trade solidarity existing between printers and publishers of politically dissident material—both male and female—and describes the role played by newspaper women in the popularization of a liberal, enlightened ideology. Margaret Jacob also describes an Enlightenment experienced by working women—the actresses of the Comédie Française. These actresses certainly displayed the solidarity of working women, as did Hunt's publishers; they also displayed a visionary sense of social relations, and of the relationship of work to social and spiritual creativity, that was unique for their time.

Who was better off—the eighteenth century intellectual whose writing and behavior were constrained by 'modern' notions of rational adulthood but who was also immune from accusations of witchcraft, or the seventeenth century visionary who was constrained to behave in an eccentric manner in order to convince her audience that she was a true prophet? In many ways the earlier period may have been a more habitable time for some women, in terms of the possible range of self-expression and public esteem available to them, than the Enlightenment. More women may have had professional careers in the 18th century, and certainly more women were writing for a living, but they were doing it with new limitations. For women's public life in the eighteenth century often seems to have been achieved at the cost of family ties (as in the case of Mary Astell), of social respectability (the actresses who joined the masonic lodge), or of physical security (the mercuries and hawkers who were vulnerable to police harrassment). Even the spunky, independent women involved in the British publishing trades did not have real economic autonomy; Margaret Hunt points out that their status was usually the result of widowhood or membership in a publishing family. She also points out that the entire phenomenon of women in publishing was short-lived; by 1750 female mercuries had almost disappeared from an increasingly rationalized industry.

The essays in this volume teach us that women did have an Enlightenment of sorts, but that the impact of Enlightenment values on the world of women was at least partly negative. Insofar as they internalized contemporary notions of the right boundaries for acceptable public behavior, enlightened women acquired a new form of symbolic baggage that women today are only just beginning to examine. The concern of many eighteenth century women to cultivate the traits of restraint and rationality of the expense of the more 'feminine' qualities of enthusiasm and spiritual ardor may account for the ongoing appeal of religion for many modern feminists, who look to myths of a matriarchal Eden or of God the Mother, and seek richer self-images by elevating the mundane activities of nurturance to cosmic proportions. The persistence of Enlightenment values may also contribute to the difficulty experienced by many other feminist thinkers of taking traditionally feminine attributes as seriously as those traditionally assigned to men. In our current preoccupation with bourgeois status and intellectual respectability, as well as our skittishness about the issues of motherhood and other 'natural' feminine impulses and activities, we are all of us, for better or worse, daughters of the Enlightenment.

NOTES

1. Elizabeth Poole, "A vision: wherein is manisfested the disease and cure of the Kingdome," (London, 1648), p. 6. On patriarchal political theory, see Jean Bethke Ehlstain, *Public Man, Private Woman. Women in Social and Political Thought.* (Princeton, 1981), Ch. 3.

2. Hilda Smith, "Gynecology and Ideology in Seventeenth Century England," *Liberating Women's History*, ed. Berenice A. Carroll, (Urbana, 1976), pp. 97-115.

3. Daniel Rogers, *Matrimoniall Honour: or, the mutuall Crowne and comfort of godly, loyall, and chaste Marriage*, (London, 1642), p. 309.

4. On women as prophets, see Phyllis Mack, "Women as Prophets during the English Civil War," *Feminist Studies*, Vol. 8, No. 1 (Spring, 1982), pp. 19-47. On Jane Lead, see Catherine F. Smith, "Women, Property, and Prophecy in Seventeenth Century England," (unpublished paper given at the Berkshire Conference on women's history, Poughkeepsie, June, 1981).

5. Frances A. Yates, *Astraea: The Imperial Theme in the Sixteenth Century*, (Harmondsworth: Penguin Books, 1977). For an account of woman's symbolic weight as a figure of disorder, see Natalie Z. Davis, "Women on Top," *Society and Culture in Early Modern France*, (Stanford, 1975), pp. 124-152.

6. Alice Clark, *Working Life of Women in the Seventeenth Century*, (London, 1982: orig. 1919).

7. On the end of the witch craze and its relation to the scientific revolution, see Keith Thomas, *Religion and the Decline of Magic*, (N.Y., 1971), Ch. 18. Also Brian Easlea, *Witch-hunting, Magic and the New Philosophy: An Introduction to Debates of the Scientific Revolution 1450-1750*, (Sussex, 1980), Ch. 5.

8. Maurice Bloch and Jean H. Bloch, "Women and the Dialectics of Nature in Eighteenth-Century French Thought," *Nature, Culture and Gender*, eds. Carol MacCormack and Marilyn Strathern, (Cambridge: Cambridge U. Press, 1980), pp. 25-42. Also see L.J. Jordanova, "Natural Facts: A Historical Perspective on Science and Sexuality, *Nature, Culture and Gender*, pp. 42-70. On the notion of Credit as a woman, see J.G.A. Pocock, "Modes of Political and Historical Time in Early 18th Century England," *Studies in Eighteenth Century Culture*, 5(1976), pp. 87-102. "She (Credit-finance) stands for that future which can only be sought passionately and inconstantly, and for the hysterical fluctuations of the urge towards it." (p. 98).

9. For a general survey of the philosophes' attitude with regard to women (mostly negative), see Abby R. Kleinbaum, "Women in the Age of Light," *Becoming Visible: Women in European History*, eds. Renate Bridenthal and Claudia Koonz, (N.Y., 1977), pp. 217-236.

10. Michel Foucault, *The History of Sexuality*, Vol I., trans. Robert Hurley, (N.Y., 1978).

11. Mack, "Women as Prophets," pp. 37-8.

12. Jonaathan Swift, *A Tale of a Tub*, ed. A.C. Guthkelch and D. Nichol Smith, 2nd ed., (Oxford: At the Clarendon Press, 1958), pp. 162-180. Quoted in Charles Cherry, "Quakers and Enthusiasts," unpublished mss., p. 33.

13. On the Shakers, see Edward Deming Andrews, *The People Called Shakers*, (N.Y., 1963), Ch. 1.

14. Jordanova, p. 61.

15. Joseph Addison, *The Spectator*, (No. 201, Saturday, October 20, 1711), quoted in Cherry, p. 33. On "masculine science," see Jordanova, pp. 45f. On political theory, see Ehlstain, Ch. 3. Ehlstain analyzes ". . . the split in Lockean epistemology between reason as formal rationality and passion as scarcely contained desire, . . . (which) *require* a public-private split, . . . one that allows human beings to exist in two divergent spheres . . ." (p. 117).

16. See Margaret Jacob's article.

17. On women writers in the 18th century, see Robert Halsband, "Women and Literature in Eighteenth Century England," *Woman in the Eighteenth Century and Other Essays*, eds. Paul Fritz and Richard Morton, (Toronto and Sarasota, 1976), pp. 55-71. Pocock writes that, "The Augustan political journalists—Defoe, Steele, Addison, Mandeville—display an uneasy concern with the increasingly visible public role of women . . ." (p. 98).

18. Perry, see Margaret Jacob's article.

19. On Anne Conway, see Carolyn Merchant, *The Death of Nature. Women, Ecology and the Scientific Revolution*, (San Francisco, 1980) pp. 253-268.

20. On the bluestockings, see Evelyn Gordon Bodek, "Salonières and Bluestockings: Educated Obsolescence and Germinating Feminism," *Feminist Studies*, Vol. 3, No. 3/4 (Spring-Summer 1976), pp. 185-199. In many ways the "Blues" mirrored Astell's ascetic values; they avoided rich food, wore plain clothes, and scorned the pursuit of pleasure.

Mary Astell's Response
to the Enlightenment

Ruth Perry

All of the contradictions of the period we call "The Enlighten-ment" were embodied in the life and writings of Mary Astell, a feminist intellectual who lived from 1666 to 1731. She argued for the rights of women yet she upheld absolute monarchy in the state. She believed in Reason but distrusted the materialism of the new way of ideas. An extremely devout Anglican, she rigorously ob-served all the vigils, fasts, and feasts of the established church. Yet her notion of heaven was a rationalist's notion: a place where all knowledge was complete, all mysteries made clear. "Poor we that toil in Life's hard drudgerie," she poeticized as a young woman, "Pick scraps of Knowledge here and there,/ While the blest Souls above do all things know. . . ." To be in heaven must include being as learned as one wished to be, she thought, dwell-ing in a culture which increasingly valued knowledge as an instru-mental means to power, but which steadfastly refused to educate its women. So she concluded that learning of an incomplete, par-tial sort was just one more of the imperfections of the earthly, mortal existence; but surely in the external afterlife that aspect of life was perfected too.

Astell was the daughter of a Newcastle coal merchant, educated in the way that women of her time were educated—the rudiments taught at home by her mother, and the rest picked up by solitary reading. In Mary Astell's case, there was also a bachelor uncle, a local clergyman named Ralph Astell, who is supposed to have had a hand in her education. Like all autodidacts, she was an insatiable reader in the particular areas she marked off as her own speciali-ties. She preferred abstract theological and philosophical argument to polite literature; she wanted to understand her place in the cos-mos more than she wanted to read romances or pastorals. She did

Ruth Perry teaches at Massachusetts Institute of Technology.

not care one whit for love, it seems; and she valued the life of the mind more than the life of the body. All sensuousness was indulged at the expense of rationality, she felt; the two modes were mutually exclusive.

Mary Astell never married, but lived by herself in a little house in Chelsea, on the outskirts of London. There she carried on an active social involvement with her many friends and acquaintances, read widely, and wrote poems, letters, essays, and polemical high church pamphlets and Tory tracts. In the fifteen years from the ages of twenty-eight to forty-three, the celebrated Mrs. Astell (for she was always granted the honorific "Mrs.") wrote six books and two rather long pamphlets: *A Serious Proposal To the Ladies, for the Advancement of their True and Greatest Interest, &c* (1694); *A Serious Proposal to the Ladies, Part the Second: Wherein a Method is offer'd for the Improvement of their Minds* (1697); *Letters Concerning the Love of God*, with John Norris (1695); *Some Reflections Upon Marriage* (1700); *Moderation Truly Stated: or, A Review of a Late Pamphlet Entitul'd Moderation a Vertue* (1704); *An Impartial Enquiry Into the Causes of Rebellion and Civil War in this Kingdom* (1704); *A Fair Way with the Dissenters and their Patrons* (1704); *The Christian Religion as Profess'd by a Daughter of the Church of England* (1705); and in 1709, *An Enquiry After Wit*, a counterblast to Shaftesbury's *A Letter Concerning Enthusiasm*. She was considered remarkable—"ingenious" was the epithet most commonly used in those days—by all who knew her.

Her books are a curious mixture of the progressive and the reactionary. She read widely in the current works of philosophy, theology, and history—both Whig and Tory, high church and latitudinarian—and peppered her writing with scores of references to them. She was learned and argumentative, and extremely involved with contemporary thought and events. Thus far she seems very much an Enlightenment figure. But her positions were often less than enlightened and seemed anachronistically to come from the ideology of an earlier age. For example, she believed in the divine right of kings to rule absolutely, and urged that no one exceed a merely passive resistance even when confronted with out-and-out tyranny. On the other hand, in the private sphere, she believed in women's right to direct their own lives and wrote against men's tyranny over women in the marriage relation. She subscribed to the Enlightenment ideal of Universal Reason—that all people were endowed by their Creator with the capacity for thought. But this divinely granted Reason was to be directed first at understanding religious concepts and used in the service of straining to understand God, rather than set to work tabulating species of plants and animals, charting the movements of the planets, poring over the reports of world travelers, or any of the more practical uses to which the enthroned Reason of the Enlightenment was put.

Although it was the democratic temper of the times in which she lived that encouraged Astell, a woman, to take up cudgels in the great public pamphlet debates over Occasional Conformity, the stand she took on that issue was elitist, anti-democratic, exclusive. She opposed democratic processes as irrelevant to abstract justice, and consciously defended the class structure as it existed in the England of her day. In fact, it is fair to say that she derived her psychic strength from this class structure, and that standing upon its firm ground enabled her to tug at the well-constructed edifice of power relations between men and women. Although her family of origin no longer had wealth, they had a pedigree, and Mary Astell considered that she had been born a gentlewoman, even if her father had made his living from the revenues of the coal trade. She expected the world to honor her for her birth and was appalled to be dismissed as a mere woman. She had great intelligence and immense ambition, but there was nowhere to direct them except into an aggressive self-abnegation. It was her anger at this situation that made her militantly vocal on the subject of equality between the sexes.

What strikes one about her life and work as a whole, what marks her as a woman of the Enlightenment, is her unqualified belief in right Reason and the faith she reposed—both personally and ideologically—in the mind. She had a lonely and difficult life, and through it all seems to have found her most continuous and sustained source of pleasure in her own mind. Whatever high hopes she had when she came to London in her early twenties, she soon found herself friendless and destitute and forced to throw herself on the charity of strangers. In those early years she learned that her active mind was her only treasure and that intellectual discourse with others was the most satisfying mode of contact available to her, a single woman without family or connections.

An example of this reaching out with the mind is a letter she wrote in 1693 to John Norris, the best known Platonist philosopher of his day, a man known for having criticized Locke for relegating to God an insufficiently important role in his explorations of the way human sensations build into ideas. Mary Astell approached Norris boldly, as an intellectual equal. She had read his work and wanted to point out an inconsistency she had discovered in the third volume of his *Discourses*. He had argued there, she said, that people ought to love God as the efficient cause of all their pleasure. Astell, who had been living on her own in London for six years by that time, and suffering privations of the spirit as well as of the body, remarked to Norris that it appeared to her that as God was the efficient cause of *all* sensation—pain as well as pleasure—one was forced to the unhappy conclusion that given His responsibility for it, pain may in fact do one good. Therefore, one could not love Him merely because He was the cause of all pleasure—as Norris had stated.[1]

She offered the correction with relish. It was her favorite form of discourse—philosophizing on religious subjects. Furthermore, questions about the place of suffering in mortal life or the love that all people owe to God were her favorite questions. Norris, who had no way of knowing this, was astonished by the clarity and force of her argument. He answered with wonder "to see such a Letter from a Woman," adding, "I find you thoroughly comprehend the Argument of my Discourse in that you have pitch'd upon the only material Objection to which it is liable . . ."[2] He then hastened to defend and clarify his line of argument, and, curious to find out what else this extraordinary woman had to say, asked her to elaborate for him the rest of her views on religion and the love of God, and the implications of these concepts for human life.

Astell's response was prompt and to the point. She believed in the power and responsibility of Reason to ascertain the moral essence of ordinary experience which proceeded from God, by logically thinking through to the abstract ideas of Justice, Goodness, Honor, etc., then trying to guide one's actions in these terms. The appetites and senses had a different purpose, she maintained; they were to preserve the body. They could not be trusted to assess the spiritual meaning of experience; steady Reason was the only proper instrument for determining Truth. To this way of thinking, the power of the mind was of the utmost importance. Since it alone could abstract moral truths from the material world, it alone could lay bare the innate ideas which lay behind one's experience; it alone could lead one to God. Nothing, for instance, could be judged properly or even understood about human life on the basis of bodily sensations alone. The true nature of experience could be ascertained only by considering its relation to the ultimate purpose of life—the contemplation of Good, Charity, Justice, etc., and the love of God. Therefore, everything was secondary to training and purifying the mind for these higher purposes: "the Mind being the Man, nothing is truly and properly his Good or Evil, but as it respects his Mind . . ." wrote Astell.[3]

This explains, in part, why Mary Astell defended so fiercely her own intellectual powers and those of all women against belittling criticism: in a universe governed by moral considerations, the ability to think clearly to the very center of things, to weigh ethical choice, was not merely an academic luxury, but crucial to one's spiritual salvation. One had to ascertain the moral Truth before one could follow it: "Clearness of Head . . . is necessary to th' obtaining Purity of Heart."[4] One's reason was one's only ladder to Heaven, and the improving and strengthening of it a religious act.

It is no wonder, then, that the first subject on which Mary Astell published was the need for women's education. *A Serious Proposal to the Ladies* (1694) was her most popular book; it went through four editions by 1697. In it she tried to persuade an audience of wealthy, unmarried women to join together and pool their dowries in order to finance collective ventures for mutual education—something like women's residential colleges. She imagined these places as little communities of women, as havens from the pressures of the marriage market, and so she stated her proposal in the form of a plea for an alternative society for unmarried women as well as an argument for women's intellectual equality.

In 1697 she published a second part to *A Serious Proposal To The Ladies*. Its starting premise was that since no one had followed her suggestion to institute schools in which women could train their minds, she thought it incumbent upon her to write a manual for thinking, a kind of "how-to-do-it" book to be used at home, for those who wanted to improve their natural reasoning capacities. For those eager but uneducated women, Mary Astell distilled books which had guided several generations of philosophers such as *Les Principes de la Philosophie de M. Descartes* and Antoine Arnauld's *L'Art de Penser*, laying out step-by-step the methods which these thinkers claimed were necessary to attain truth.

She warned that clearing the mind of distractions and misconceptions was no easy matter. "They who apply themselves to the Contemplation of Truth, will perhaps at first find a Contraction or

Emptiness of Thought, and that their Mind offers nothing on the Subject they wou'd consider . . . and tho' not empty of all Thought, yet Thinks nothing clearly or to the purpose."[5] One had to begin with a meditative shedding of worldly attachments.

> We can neither Observe the Errors of our Intellect, nor the Ir-regularity of our Morals whilst we are darkened by Fumes, agitated with unruly Passions, or carried away with eager De-sires after Sensible things and vanities. We must therefore withdraw our Minds from the World, from adhering to the Senses, from the Love of Material Beings, of Pomps and Gaities; for 'tis these that usually Steal away the Heart, that seduce the Mind to such unaccountable Wanderings, and so fill up its Capacity that they leave no room for Truth . . .[6]

She felt that women, raised to be playthings or drudges, their lives filled with distraction and frivolity, were particularly susceptible to these "Fumes" and "eager Desires," "Pomps and Gaities." They stood in special need of disciplined thought as a kind of machete to hack through the underbursh of false ideas and corrupt values which always surrounded them. Ideas firmly rooted in sensation were, like weeds, hard to extirpate; as Locke had demonstrated, that was the common soil in which they grew. "For tho we are ac-quainted with the Sound of some certain words, e.g. *God, Reli-gion, Pleasure* and *Pain, Honor* and *Dishonour*, and the like," she wrote, "yet having no other *Ideas* but what are convey'd to us by these Trifles we converse with, we frame to ourselves strange and awkward notions of them, comfortable only to those *Ideas* sensa-tion had furnish'd us with, which sometimes grew so strong and fixt, that 'tis scarce possible to introduce a new Scheme of Thoughts, and so to disabuse us, especially whilst these Objects are thick about us."[7] A woman without any other basis for under-standing "who sees her self and others respected in proportion to that Pomp and Bustle they make in the world, will form her Idea of Honour accordingly,"[8] she explained.

> When a poor Young Lady is taught to value her self on nothing but her Cloaths, and to think she's very fine when well accoutred. When she hears say that 'tis Wisdom enough for her to know how to dress her self, that she may become amiable in his eyes, to whom it appertains to be knowing and

learned; who can blame her if she lay out her Industry and money on such Accomplishments, and sometimes extends it farther than her misinformer desires she should? . . . What tho' she be sometimes told of another World, she has however a more lively perception of this, and may well think, that if her Instructors were in earnest when they tell her of *hereafter*, they would not be so busied and concerned about what happens *here*.[9]

One had to make a clearing, to begin as Descartes did in his warm Bavarian farmhouse, locked away from the temptations and distractions of the world in comfortable isolation. Astell herself spent many hours every day alone in silent thought and meditation. Everywhere in her writings there is an awareness of the preciousness of time and an injunction not to waste it in mere social bustle and activity.

Norris may have introduced Astell to Descartes, as he surely urged her to read Antoine Arnauld's *L'Art de Penser* (1662). Sometimes referred to as "The Port Royal Logic", this book had gone through six French editions and three English editions by the time *A Serious Proposal to The Ladies Part II* was published, the earliest in 1674 at the urging of John Locke and with the "recommendation and approbation" of the Royal Society of London.[10] In their published letters, Norris also recommends to Astell the works of a number of other systematizing French philosophers of the seventeenth century: Sylvain Régis' *Systeme de Philosophie* (1690) and Nicholas Malebranche's *Recherche de la Vérité (1674)*.[11] But M. Arnauld's *L'Art de Penser* was the book which most affected Astell's sense of what was involved in thinking clearly and systematically.

The second part of *A Serious Proposal to The Ladies*, then, demonstrates the influence that John Norris exercised over Astell at this point in her career. Indeed, her book might be read as a training manual for Norris' brand of Christian platonism. Certainly it incorporates the notions of those thinkers who had been seminal for Norris, whom he always recommended for beginners: Descartes, Malebranche, and, above all, Antoine Arnauld. But Astell prepared their ideas for an audience of uneducated women and presented the methods rather more schematically than one finds in the original. Much of *A Serious Proposal to The Ladies Part II* is a précis or paraphrase of what Arnauld had outlined, in textbook fashion, as the steps for rigorous thought. Arnauld had written *L'Art de Penser* quickly, on a dare, as a summary of everything an amateur philosopher might need to know for clear, logical, step-by-step thinking. It quickly became a method book, the handbook for every philosopher of that century. Its impulse was practical, pedagogical. It gave Astell the system she was looking for, and at the same time verified her earlier conviction that a trained mind, because it clarified human choice, was necessary to secular and religious welfare alike.

Arnauld had argued that ideas were not respresentative (Platonic) entities, but merely the perceptual or cognitive acts of limited and finite beings, and therefore they had to be tested and examined before they could be relied upon. In discussing this process of test and examination, in giving instruction for the cultivation of the mind, he anticipated many of the epistemological questions that were to come out of eighteenth-century empiricism: how ideas arise; what are the relations between these ideas and the "reality" which initiates them, the "reality" we think of as visible in the material world; and finally, what is the degree of certainty of our knowledge. Arnauld was not interested in these questions as epistemological paradoxes, as later philosophers have been. He deemed his enterprise useful for other reasons, most particularly because he thought that the mind *could* perceive truth, if only it was properly trained.

> Nothing is more to be esteemed than aptness in discerning the true from the false. Other qualities of mind are of limited use, but precision of thought is essential to every aspect and walk of life. To distinguish truth from error is difficult not only in the sciences but also in the everyday affairs that men engage in and discuss. Men are everywhere confronted with alternative routes—some true and others false—and reason must choose between them. Who chooses well has a sound mind; who chooses ill, a defective one. Capacity for discerning the Truth is the most important measure of men's minds.
>
> Our principal task is to train the judgment, rendering it as exact as we can. To this end the greatest part of our studies should be devoted.
>
> We are accustomed to use reason as an instrument for acquiring the sciences, but we ought to use the sciences as an instrument for perfecting the reason: Accuracy of mind is in-

finitely more important than any speculative knowledge acquired from the truest and most established sciences.[12]

Astell followed this line closely, although she emphasized less the need for an acute mind to distinguish true from false in "everyday affairs" and public life ("Men are everywhere confronted with alternative routes") and was more concerned with everyone's private responsibility for living a principled life—and struck with the impossibility of doing so without a good understanding of moral reasoning.

> . . . everyone who pretends to Reason, who is a Voluntary Agent and therefore Worthy of Praise or Blame, Reward or Punishment, must *Chuse* his Actions and determine his Will to that Choice by some Reasonings or Principles either true or false, and in proportion to his Principles and the Consequences he deduces from them he is to be accounted, if they are Right and Conclusive a Wise Man, if Evil, Rash and Injudicious a Fool. If then it be the property of Rational Creatures, and Essential to their very Natures to Chuse their Actions, and to determine their Wills to that Choice by such Principles and Reasonings as their Understandings are furnish'd with, they who are desirous to be rank'd in that Order of Beings must conduct their Lives by these Measures, begin with their Intellectuals, inform themselves what are the plain and first Principles of Action and Act accordingly.[13]

To think properly about the "plain and first Principles of Action", one had to learn to use language accurately and to clarify one's terms first, by separating and distinguishing the ideas annexed to each word. "Thus many times our Ideas are thought to be false when the fault is really in our Language, we make use of Words without joyning any, or only loose and indeterminate Ideas to them, Prating like Parrots who can Modify Sounds, and Pronounce Syllables . . ."[14] She warned her women readers to pay particular attention to their use of "particles"—what we call conjunctions—the words which provide the connections among ideas. She advised them to read Locke's section on "particles" in Book III of the *Essay on Human Understanding*. She stressed accuracy in the use of this part of speech, because although she did not think women as illiterate as generally they were thought to

be—and was convinced that they often pretended to spell worse
than they knew how in order to avoid being called proud, pedantic, or unwomanly—still, she believed that the grammatical mistake women were most commonly prey to was the misuse of "particles" or conjunctions, which denoted the relationship between
clauses and therefore between ideas.

She agreed with Arnauld that the mind followed a natural course
in reasoning; this, of course, was another proof that human beings
with minds were *intended* to think.[15] Her method built upon this
natural capacity, and its steps were an amalgam of Descartes'
Rules for the Direction of the Mind and the Port Royal Logic reworked into five parts: 1) define the questions and the terms; 2)
weed out all issues which are not directly connected to the matter
under consideration; 3) proceed in an orderly fashion; 4) examine
every aspect of the subject; subdivide the question into as many
parts as is necessary for perfect understanding; 5) judge no farther
than you perceive; take nothing for truth that has not been proved.

After setting out these rules with many qualifications and examples, Astell demonstrated the method practically, taking as her
sample questions the old conundrums of whether or not there was
a God or a Perfect Being, and whether or not a rich man was nec-
essarily a happy man. The import of her discussion was, as usual,
to show that the truth which could be arrived at by a series of logical steps was often counter-intuitive. That is, one could prove the
existence of God even if He was not available to the senses; and
wealth was not a necessary or sufficient condition for happiness although worldly wisdom deemed it so. In part this was a purely abstract position, derived ultimately from Plato, with a heavy dose of
Cartesian rationalism. But in part it was psychological protection
against a universe of thought which took women to be inferior to
men in intellect, moral judgment, and perception. To reason from
abstract principles rather than from "things as they are", was to ignore the bias of the social world, to invest the solitary thinking
mind with the capacity to arrive at truth regardless of education or
experience, and, for a woman, to thus be elevated to equality with
men in one swift movement.

This then, was the starting place for Astell's feminism: a belief
in an immaterial intellect which had no gender but was an essential
feature of all human nature, and whose purpose was to discover
and articulate nature and moral principles abstracted from the im-
perfect world. Because she believed in a firm and immutable

Truth, which all minds were capable of reaching given time and training, it followed that women were equal to men in the only respect that mattered. The miracle of reason itself seemed to bless her logic, for surely that marvelous faculty was a sign of something "too Divine, to have it once imagin'd that it was made for nothing else but to move a portion of Matter 70 or 80 Years".[16] Everything in the divinely ordered universe had an end or purpose for which it was fitted and predestined, and human beings with their extraordinary faculties were obviously meant to engage in philosophic pursuits, so that they might discover and disseminate Truth.

> For, since GOD has given Women as well as Men intelligent Souls, why should they be forbidden to improve them? Since he has not denied us the faculty of Thinking, why Shou'd we not (at least in gratitude to Him) employ our Thoughts on Himself their noblest Object, and not unworthily bestow them on Trifles and Gaities and secular Affairs? Being the Soul was created for the contemplation of Truth, as well as for the fruition of Good, is it not as cruel and unjust to exclude Women from the knowledge of the one, as well as from the enjoyment of the other? Especially since the Will is blind, and cannot chuse but the direction of the Understanding; or to speak more properly, since the Soul always *Wills* according as she *Understands,* so that if she *Understands* amiss, she *Wills* amiss: And as Exercise enlarges and exalts any Faculty, so thro' want of using, it becomes crampt and lessened; if we make little or no use of our Understandings we shall shortly have none to use; and the more contracted, and unemploy'd the deliberating and directive Power is, the more liabile is the elective to unworthy and mischievious options.[17]

One of the unmistakable signs of this divine gift, to Mary Astell's mind, was her own uplifting ambition, a powerful yearning to work toward some worthwhile goal, to employ her thoughts on the noblest objects rather than to "unworthily bestow them on Trifles and Gaities and secular Affairs." This idealistic urge—which in overly-protected and unworldly women is uncertain of how to find and devote itself to the "noblest object"—has been brilliantly described by George Eliot in the person of her thwarted heroine of

Middlemarch, Dorothea Brooke. The description of this woman, ardent and striving, puts one in mind of Mary Astell. George Eliot's depiction of the elder Miss Brooke's solitary reading, her religious bent, her scorn for the usual women's frivolities, is a picture whose essential outline delineates an important aspect of this intellectual woman of an earlier time. With an accurate intuition, Eliot has her heroine image herself born in the seventeenth century. "Could I not learn to read Latin and Greek aloud to you," she asks her pedantic husband-to-be, "as Milton's daughters did to their father, without understanding what they read?" Like Mary Astell, Dorothea fed her spiritual hunger on treatises, particularly those of fervent writers who described their struggles for faith in the face of the growing materialism of the seventeenth century. Like George Eliot's Dorothea Brooke, Mary Astell "knew many passages of Pascal's Pensees and of Jeremy Taylor's by heart; and to her the destinies of mankind, seen by the light of Christianity, made the solicitudes of feminine fashion appear an occupation for Bedlam." Eliot continues: "She could not reconcile the anxieties of the spiritual life involving eternal consequences, with a keen interest in guimp and artificial protrusions of drapery. Her mind was theoretic, and yearned by its nature after some lofty conception . . ."[18] Like Dorothea Brooke, Mary Astell was driven by a powerful ambition to turn her idealism and youthful energy to account for mankind, all the while conscious of the anomaly of these sentiments in a woman's breast.

When she was eighteen, she wrote these self-conscious lines about her ambition, identifying it as that more-than-mortal aspect of herself which must have come from God or the "first mover."

> What's this that with such vigour fills my breast?
>   Like the first mover finds no rest,
>   And with it's force dos all things draw,
> Makes all submit to its imperial Law!
> Sure 'tis a spark 'bove what Prometheus stole,
>   Kindled by a heav'nly coal,
>   Their sophistry I can controul,
> Who falsely say that women have no soul.

The poem goes on to say that she is not ambitious for the usual things, for land or titles, wealth or fame, things which a woman she had no way of attaining in any case. Her ambition is for a

"Crown of Glory," a figure of speech implying both heavenly reward and the martyrdom of the crown of thorns, the perfect combination of faith and humility. "I scorn to weep for Worlds" she wrote from her front parlour, never noting the ironies of the male military images,

> . . . May I by reign
> And Empire o're my self obtain,
> In Caesars throne I'de not sit down
> Nor wou'd I stoop for Alexanders Crown.

It was her standard paradox, the inverse relation of the worldly to the divine: the more substantial the material rewards, the less valuable the spiritual gains. The reason for teaching women how to think was so that they might be able to distinguish between the motives of this world and the next. The vision had to be retrained, so to speak, so that one could distinguish the true Good and make life choices accordingly. Reason was to be exercised in the service of spiritual improvement.

As I have suggested, Astell's insistence on sweeping away material considerations was in part motivated by a desire to put men and women on an equal footing before God. And indeed, when looked at closely, what Astell claimed about equal educational opportunities for women was very different from what others said who wrote about the subject.[19] It was generally held that women's minds were inferior to men's minds—or at least different from them. The usual reasons for educating women did not include making great scholars or artists of them, but only making them fit company for men and capable of educating their children in rudimentary literacy. These claims often entailed an argument against the current prejudice that education rendered women unfit for marriage and domesticity, or that it weakened their morals, or both.

Astell never merely argued with the other "educationalists" that women had a right to an education. She also criticized the social institutions (schools, marriage) which thwarted women's intellectual ambition and thereby prevented their most important human function. She was convinced that women's intellectual shortcomings were entirely due to social prejudice and lack of training, rather than to anything innate. "So partial are Men as to expect Brick where they afford no straw," she said.[20] This was a very different message from that broadcast by other "educationalists" of the seventeenth century. She recognized that the attitude towards gender in her society was oppressive; she was not simply in favor of extending the opportunity for formal learning to more people. She thought the potential and capabilities of the female mind and spirit had to be completely reassessed.

This insistence on an extended vision of human rights and recognition of a wider equality is certainly consistent with the spreading democratic ideals of the Enlightenment. But Astell stopped with herself. As I mentioned earlier, she saw nothing wrong with a class-stratified society or with an inherited hierarchy in the state. Her women's colleges were intended for upper-class women—at most for "decayed gentlewomen"—and not for women from the lower ranks of the social order. To be fair, it must be noted that in 1709 she helped to set up a school at the Royal Hospital in Chelsea for the poor daughters of outpensioners, veterans of England's foreign wars. That is, she crusaded for literacy for women, even poor women. But her irritation at sex prejudice did not extend to class prejudice, and she never breathed a word to undermine privilege. The friend whom she appointed her executrix had been a slave-owner, a fact which they both probably took for granted without discomfort. Her associates and patrons were wealthy and pious women from the highest circles of the aristocracy, women who supported her financially; she was very respectful of their status. In various places in her writings one hears a note of smug, self-congratulatory class consciousness, as when she eulogizes the gentry and sneers at the "rabble"—hardly the tone of the democratic political rhetoric of the Enlightenment.

In terms of national politics, too, Astell's attitudes are more easily characterized as counter-Enlightenment. For one thing, she was an ardent monarchist, resisting every step of the way the progressive pull of the seventeenth century towards republican government. She thought the emphasis on individual liberty rather than on the prerogatives of the monarch was an extremely dangerous tendency. A king had to embody certain unwavering principles, she said; he could not be responsible to the passion and folly of each man in his kingdom. In a state which allowed authority to be questioned it was unavoidable that strong and cunning men would successively usurp the power of the state for their own ends, "under the specious Pretences of the People's Rights and Liberties."[21] This is what had happened, she felt, in the Civil War, and she could cite Clarendon chapter and verse on the details.[22] Although she conceded Locke's genius, she disagreed with him on this as on everything else. In this famous *Two Treatises of Government*, written circa 1682 but published anonymously the year after the Glorious Revolution, he described government as a voluntary association among free men to better preserve their lives, liberties, and property. If the government did not answer these needs of its people, he asserted, the people had the right to seek another.[23] Mary Astell countered: "The people have no Authority over their own Lives, consequently they don't invest such an Authority in their Governours."[24]

Mary Astell held that the laws of God and man required unquestioning obedience to ordained authority at all times. Civil peace and prosperity in a kingdom depended upon this unshakeable rule, for otherwise subjects spent all their energies dealing with power—whether seizing it or protecting it—rather than in more constructive and productive pursuits. Rulers, Astell thought, had a duty to "vigorously exert that lawful Authority *GOD* had given them" and to prevent rebels from infecting the minds of their people "with evil Principles and Representations, with Speeches that have double Meanings and equivocal Expressions, *Innuendo's*, and secret Hints and Insinuations."[25] A free press and a free pulpit produced a factionalized, dissatisfied, rebellious population, she thought: no sensible government could afford to permit slander and subversion to go unchecked.

This insistence on intellectual coercion is an unexpected turn for a woman who placed so much emphasis on right Reason, who believed that the mind had a natural affinity for truth and that the Universe was governed by Intelligence. Yet Astell agreed with Swift's Brobdingnagian king who "knew no reason why those who entertain opinions prejudicial to the public be obliged to change, or should not be obliged to conceal them. . . . For a man may be allowed to keep poisons in his closets, but not to vend them about as cordials."[26] She thought that anonymous political pamphlets ought to be outlawed and that critics of the monarchy or of the established church ought to be forced to acknowledge the views they printed, in broad daylight as it were, and to be punished accordingly. As Bolingbroke stated it: the "good of society may require that no person be deprived of the protection of the government on account of his options in religious matters," but it did not follow

that "men ought to be trusted in any degree with the preservation
of the establishment, who must, to be consistent with their principles, endeavor the subversion of what is established."[27]

She believed that authority needed to be respected, right or
wrong, and that even when rulers behaved contrarily to the dictates
of sense or religion, a loyal subject was bound to accord them at
least a "passive obedience." This was the byword of the conservative Tory position in the reign of William and Mary, and it implied
that even if James II had been an impossible monarch, the citizenry
had no right to depose him. It was often accompanied by a belief
in "passive resistance," a kind of latter-day conscientious objection. One could refuse to obey intolerable commands—the way
the Anglican clergy refused to read James' Declaration from the
pulpit—but one could not rebel or actively oppose the divinely appointed sovereign. Those who held to this doctrine after the events
of 1688 were distinctly High Tory, and some of them extended
their principled resistance by refusing to endorse oaths of loyalty
to William and Mary. These non-jurors, as they were called, believed that their oaths of loyalty to James II could not be retracted
while he lived, nor superseded by oaths to a "usurper." Many non-
jurors lost their positions in the church or the universities because
of their stands, much as American academics in the 1950s suffered
consequences for openly refusing to sign loyalty oaths. Theirs was
a non-violent refusal to comply with the government, a conservative alternative to the solution offered by Locke and other political
thinkers, who claimed that the people had the right to overthrow
the government when it did not answer their needs, and reinstate
another that did.

Those who believed in passive obedience insisted that one could
only resist the government in non-violent ways, because anything
more was a crime against divinely ordained succession and so ultimately a crime against God. As such, the doctrine implied a total
belief in the jurisdictional rights of one's governors, even though
one ultimately had to consult one's own conscience on moral questions. It assumed no responsibility on the part of the government
towards the governed, and implied that subjects ought never actively question or resist, let alone violently contest, the dictates of
their rulers. Locke sneered at it as a political solution: "Who
would not think it an admirable peace betwixt the mighty and the
mean when the lamb without resistance yielded his throat to
be torn by the imperious wolf? . . . no doubt Ulysses, who was a

prudent man, preached up passive obedience, and exhorted his company to a quiet submission by representing to them of what concernment peace was to mankind, and by showing the inconveniences which might happen if they should offer to resist Polyphemous, who had not the power over them."[28]

Astell would have argued that Polyphemous was far from being a lawfully constituted authority.

Mary Astell was twenty-two at the time of the Glorious Revolution, and what it had meant to her was that violence and disorder were part and parcel of political change. For over a year her native city of Newcastle had been riven with riots, conspiracies, charges and countercharges. A few months after William and Mary were crowned, a rioting mob (infiltrated, they said, by rebellious covenanters from across the Scottish border) tore up the fine new bronze statue of James II from the center of town, and threw it into the Tyne. Astell's family had been outraged, as were all the families of the coal barons, for they remained steadfastly loyal as a group to the Stuarts. For the rest of her life, Mary Astell maintained that chaos and violence were the inevitable effects of tampering with monarchical succession. Factionalism always brought discontent and conspiracy.

She took the concomitant stand against religious toleration. Open dissent had dangerous political implications, as far as she was concerned. Because England had a national religion, the interests of the church and state could not be separated. It would start, she said, with objections to the forms of the religious service of the national church, but before long the objections would be directed at the form of government. The consequence of such disagreements was civil strife such as had threatened the country throughout the seventeenth century. These were matters too serious to be bandied about in a free marketplace of ideas.

Mary Astell's position on this question of religious toleration can be seen most clearly in her controversy with Shaftesbury over the handling of the French Huguenots in London, an issue to which he addressed himself in his *A Letter Concerning Enthusiasm* (1708), the piece which later became the first treatise of *Characteristics*. A closer look at the details of Shaftesbury's essay and at Astell's refutation of the principles he enunciates there will illustrate her "counter-Enlightenment" position, and the reasoning which lay behind it.

Originally a private letter addressed to Lord Somers, Shaftesbury's *A Letter Concerning Enthusiasm* had been occasioned by the activity of a group of French Protestant enthusiasts, known to us as "the French prophets," who had come to England seeking toleration in 1706, and had become increasingly, notoriously, public about the fits, seizures, and mystical visions which were to them the signs of their religious faith. The English, already in the throes of their own internal controversy about religious toleration—a bitter and widespread dispute over the terms of the Occasional Conformity Bill—were not receptive to such exotic religionists. No one welcomed the example of these *inspirées* with their seizures and mystical visions, who deserved sympathy for being hounded from papist France, but were more uncomfortably extreme in their religious fits than the most zealous nonconformists. Disapproving tracts, broadsides, and pamphlets against them began to appear. By 1708 they were considered so much a public nuisance by some that there was talk of silencing them legally.[29]

A Letter Concerning Enthusiasm was a generous-spirited bid for rational response to these enthusiasts. It was absurd, said Shaftesbury, to try to legislate in matters of religion any more than one would want to legislate the proper way to do mathematics, or the standards for wit. Religious fervor, he continued, was like a kind of temporary insanity, a "Pannick"—like being in love—and until it passed, the person seized by it was not likely to be able to hear any criticism. The best way to handle the distasteful excess and extravagance of the French prophets was not by withdrawing from them the rights of the famed English liberty of conscience, but by ridiculing them, exposing them to the laughter they deserved. Truth would always bear up under ridicule and the rest would simply drop away. Provided the investigation was mannerly, he said, religion could not be treated with "too much good Humor, or [examined] with too much Freedom & Familiarity." To legislate against the French prophets would elevate them to the status of martyrs, give them more attention than they merited. Why, if the Jews had only had the idea to put on puppet shows about Jesus, he went on, "I am apt to think they wou'd have done our Religion more harm, than by all their other ways of Severity."[30]

Mary Astell was appalled by Shaftesbury's attitudes when she read the piece, and after a little urging from her friends, with whom no doubt she had amply aired her opinion of these ideas, she wrote *Bart'lemy Fair: or, An Enquiry After Wit* (1709), which was her answer to this dangerous liberalism. The author was just the sort of deistical Enlightenment thinker whom Mary Astell detested. She considered his thought weak and sentimental, and dangerous to the social order. Moreover, this "letter" was catching on and having too powerful an effect among disputants in London's fashionable drawing rooms. Someone had to answer it. To begin with, she violently opposed his conception of religion. Where she believed in a personified God, an Authority to be reckoned with and treated with utmost respect, this author wrote about religion conceptually, as a set of propositions to be bought and sold in the free market-place of ideas. Furthermore, she had always considered the tenets of the established church to be logically consistent, and founded on a series of inductions, which began by assuming the centrality of human reason to the meaning of human life. And here was this writer saying that religion was a "Pannick," an ill-founded, over-heated, superstitious feeling, and that even Christianity might have been blighted in the bud if it had been subjected to ridicule in its early days. She certainly did not approve of the French prophets, but she did not think religion a fit subject for ridicule in any circumstances:

> For until this Blessed Age of *Liberty*! which has made us so much Wiser than our Fathers, and that Men of Wit, found it turn to their Account to be thought Men of Business; it was never thought a Service to the Public to expose the Establish'd Religion, no not when it was ever so false and ridiculous in it self, to the Contempt of the People.[31]

Astell did not know exactly who had written *A Letter Concerning Enthusiasm*, although she knew it was someone of an aristocratic, educated, Whiggish stamp, someone bold and confident, in sympathy with the new way of ideas, scornful of the restraints of the past, hailing liberty, and optimistic about the natural order which would be laid bare when the encrustations of custom and superstition were cleared away. It is "a very *Drawcansir* of a Book" said Mary Astell, comparing it to a burlesque swashbuckling character in a play written by George Villiers, the Duke of Buckingham, a character whose bombastic speeches and attitudinizing sword play satirized the idealized heroics of contemporary tragedies. "It *cuts and slashes* all that Men have hitherto accounted Sacred; is so *fierce a hero*, as to *fright* the *Good Christian*."[32]

Shaftesbury held that optimistic view of mankind subscribed to by forward-thinking natural philosophers of his day: that human beings left to their own devices would gradually find their way to the Good. The problem lay in repression, in external pressures which distorted the natural process. People were by nature sensible, rational beings, and if they were not manipulated sooner or later they would arrive at the Truth of any matter.

Mary Astell was disturbed by the lack of attention to any kind of self-discipline in such a formulation. ". . . in our Father's Days, excessive and unrestrain'd Liberty might perhaps be call'd Licentiousness", she reproved. She was aware that her point of view was old-fashioned, dated, and that *A Letter Concerning Enthusiasm* had been very well received by urbane Londoners: ". . . it is cry'd up as a *Non-Pariello* for Language, Thought, and all that— 'Tis industriously spread in the nation; put, by way of ABC, into the hands of every young Fellow, who begins to speak great swelling words . . . And sent, by way of Mission, into Foreign Parts. . . ." Nevertheless, these new-fangled notions held by the young Whig Lords, and the way they conducted themselves, were a betrayal of the ideas she has been brought up on.

> Our Antient *English* Peerage were of another strain; they were not more remarkable for their Loyalty to their Prince, than their Piety to their GOD. They subdu'd themselves, as well as their Enemies. Their Health was not consum'd in Debauchery, nor were their Estates squander'd in Vanity, Gaming and Luxury; but Generously bestow'd in charity, Hospitality and Liberality. Real Merit only obtain'd their Friendship; and whatever a Man's Outward Circumstances might be, if his Mind was great enough to emulate and follow, much more if it was able to set a Pattern of the most Generous, Virtuous and Noble Actions, he was duly qualify'd for their Esteem and kindness . . . They despis'd a Man who wou'd forsake his own Reason, and blindly follow other Men's; who wou'd violate his Conscience to make his Fortune or save his Estate; and who had either no Principles, or such as wou'd conform to every Fashion."[33]

This description of a mythologized English patriarchy shows Astell's basically feudal impulse when registering the changes she witnessed in her society. How could "men of wit" or "men of business" compare with such idealized integrity? Their modern "freedom" was really a kind of ignominious enslavement to the senses, to the material world, and to each other's opinions—whereas the dignified and self-regulated freedom of their forefathers had been a truer freedom of the spirit. She thought it a bad trade to exchange established institutions, faith, and stability for a Whig notion of "liberty."

The heart of her critique lay in rejecting the "state of Nature" which Shaftesbury assumed. As she pointed out, no one ever had been or ever would be as free as his line of reasoning demanded that people be. Free and impartial criticism as an intellectual process was not possible so long as the power relations among people were unequal. Rank, property and titles would have to be abolished before all ideas could be approached by the generality of humankind with the utter neutrality which his theory posited. Market-place thinking could only work in the most benign circumstances, ideal circumstances which never obtained in the real world. *"Were Matters ballanc'd*, were no other *Force* us'd but that of *Wit and Raillery, Reason wou'd* have *fair play*, Mankind wou'd *flourish. Wonderful* wou'd be the *Harmony and Temper* arising from *all these Contrarieties*, they wou'd make up that right *Humor*, which the Letter *contends* for, as going more than half way toward *Thinking rightly* of Everything." She thought his emphasis on "right *Humor*" absurd and naive, as if all the hatred and internecine fighting of English history during the seventeenth century could be attributed to the peevish petulance of men being out of humor. "And Men *being mildly treated, and let alone*," she added sarcastically, "they wou'd never Rage to that degree as to occasion *Blood-shed, Wars, Persecutions and Devastations in the World*; which proceed from nothing else but their being put out of Humor, by not being permitted to do what they will."[34]

Mary Astell's critique of Shaftesbury's liberal permissiveness was based on a profound distrust of any political solution which did not have the weight of custom, religious sanction, and absolute law behind it—such that it could withstand the vicissitudes of party politics, economic interest, and the other winds of change which blew from different directions with varying and unpredictable force, continually threatening the stability of the state. Her philosophical belief in idealized Platonic forms is consistent with her political belief in a stable ruling class which limited the political responsibility of all others in managing the affairs of the state. Reasoning from fallible, self-centered, individualized definitions

of right and wrong meant sacrificing the possibility of perfection at
the outset, whether one was trying to define absolute moral virtue
as distinct from private good, or trying to enunciate a public policy
for England which did not concern itself with the interests of separate, fragmented groups.

Her judgment was not simpleminded. She was well aware of the
nature of the problem she was grappling with. She fully understood the point of those who felt that the citizenry had the right to
make and unmake government as it answered the needs of the governed. She also responded to the pull of empiricism, the appeal of
commonsensical and verifiable truths over the abstract and the idealized. But she braced herself to resist that pull because she saw
that what these political and philosophical attitudes sacrificed to a
freeing relativity was belief in absolute authority—a belief that
was the cornerstone of an ethical system, to her mind, and the only
means to lasting civil peace.

These conclusions can hardly be called paradigms of Enlightenment thought. Whenever she had a chance, Astell attacked what
today we would call the central principles of the Enlightenment:
the rights of individuals within the state, religious toleration, and
class leveling. Instead of questioning authority, she strenuously
defended it, both on historical and theoretical grounds. She
thought of most objections to monarchical government as seditious.

Nor can she be considered a member of the other recognized intellectual camp of the English Enlightenment, the so-called Tory
satirists, which included men like Pope, Swift, Arbuthnot and
Bolingbroke. With the exception of a few points in her refutation
of Shaftesbury, she was not interested in anatomizing the limitations of the sensibility which was destroying her beloved tradition-
alism. She did not lampoon the rising commercial interests or the
materialism of the new empirical science. Although she felt called
upon the defend the disembodied, spiritual nature of the soul from
Locke's materialistic ontogeny,[35] for the most part she valued the
spirit of discovery abroad in the culture; and she bent her efforts to
reconciling the areas of religion and science by showing that they
were not mutually exclusive but explored different kinds of knowledge. Like all figures of the past, Mary Astell exhibited a mixture
of those attitudes which we have come to think of as typifying her
historical period, as well as some which seem out of joint with her
time.

I would still argue, however, that in spite of some of her anachronistic attitudes, Mary Astell must be understood as a phenomenon of the Enlightenment. That she wrote and published—if not under her own name, at least without obscuring her authorship—and maintained her respectability through it all, was a sign of the times. Women's writing for an audience larger than immediate family and friends was not really in evidence until the end of the seventeenth century or even the beginning of the eighteenth century. Although women wrote in England from the time of the Restoration—Katherine Philips and Aphra Behn wrote imaginative literature (poems, plays, and novels)—they had not formerly trespassed on the more "serious" intellectual territory men had traditionally occupied (philosophy, theology, history, and political commentary). When women wrote for public consumption in that earlier period they forfeited their reputations: they were refused access to the best drawing rooms or were stigmatized as eccentric, sexually loose, or otherwise unseemly. The fact that Mary Astell gained a following among certain aristocratic women *because* she was an author—the fact that her published work elevated her to their level and gave her a prominence which neither her birth nor her financial status could confer—is a sign of the times in which they all lived.

Intellectual activity enjoyed a new prestige in secular culture in the early eighteenth century. London was a sophisticated urban center where controversies on all subjects raged in the many journals and pamphlets for which there was a remarkably wide readership. Astell came to hold her place in that society precisely because it valued individual accomplishment, departures from tradition, and literate intellectual polemic—no matter what her own views on these matters were. One could say that the Enlightenment atmosphere drew forth and encouraged certain aspects of Astell's human repertoire: her intellectuality, her argumentativeness, and her pride in self. These qualities resonated with the *zeitgeist* even though the particular content of her own ideas ran counter to it.

None of us is immune to the spirit of the times in which we live, and Astell was no exception; she absorbed much in spite of herself. One finds, for example, the rhetorical imprint of contemporary political theory on her prose. She describes herself as an honest English subject "with an English Spirit and Genius, set out upon the Forlorn Hope, meaning no hurt to any body, not desiring any thing but the Publick Good, and to retrieve, if possible, the Native Liberty, the Rights and Privileges of the Subject."[36] Such diction, ironically enough, sounds like Locke, whom Astell had read and admired but with whom, finally, she always had to disagree. She asks: "*If* all Men are born free, *how is it that all Women are born Slaves?*"[37] These formulations were in the air, and even if her professed political sentiments ran counter to the meaning of these phrases, they seem to have affected her—as if their intellectual permissiveness encouraged her to speak out in behalf of herself and other women. Indeed, grappling with such political issues as the limits of personal liberty may have first led her to her feminist assumptions about the equality of men and women.

By seeing the realms of public and private as discontinuous, she managed to believe in both the freedom and independence of women and absolute authority in the state at the same time. The needs of one's society and their answering political institutions had ancient histories which long preceded one's own brief entrance into the world. These institutions had a prior claim to one's loyalty. One the other hand—and here is where modern feminists take exception to Astell—she assumed that a woman entered marriage with her eyes fully open, that she was a free adult and could do as she liked with her life. A woman, Astell claimed, voluntarily submitted herself to her husband's will—his was not an authority which pre-existed her. That is, one could choose one's domestic arrangements, whereas one was born into a civil state willy-nilly. In other words, marriage was like voluntarily taking out citizenship in an absolute monarchy and agreeing to comply with its laws for life. And once it was a *fait accompli*, given Astell's political ideas, there was no turning back. Still, she insisted on the irony of a double standard according to which those who were readiest to decry tyranny in the state entertained it well enough at home: "how much soever Arbitrary Power may be dislik'd on a Throne, not *Milton* himself wou'd cry up Liberty to poor *Female Slaves*, or plead for the Lawfulness of Resisting a Private Tyranny."[38]

To sum up then, Mary Astell's place in the Enlightenment is a complicated one. On the face of it she ran against the current, and yet her very existence as an intellectual and a feminist is a testimony to the values of the age. Her position as a woman of leisure permitted her the speculative mode she valued above all others. Her Reason, and the philosophic implications of that attribute, permitted her to choose a life of celibacy and devotion to study and writing. As she expressed it in a poem of 1689, the terms of that chosen life were simplicity and liberty—the avoidance of stultifying convention, and the rational use of her own time.

> O how uneasy shou'd I be,
> If tied to Custom and formalitie,
> Those necessary evils of the Great,
> Which bind their hands, and manacle their feet
> Nor Beauty, Parts, nor Portion me expose
> My most beloved Liberty to lose.
> And thanks to Heav'n my time is all my own
>   I when I please can be alone;
> Nor Company, nor Courtship to steal away.
>   That treasure they can ne'er repay.

These sentiments are reminiscent of the polite austerity and gentlemanly dedication to the muse of a poet like Abraham Cowley, an early favorite of Astell's. But the stamp of her times is to be found in the explanation of what she did with the solitude she writes about. Seventeenth-century England has many examples of religious, aristocratic women living in retirement on their estates, who praise—in letter, essay, and poem—the pleasures of religious meditation and prayer. It is the theme of numbers of poets who re-dedicate themselves to their art with periodic perorations about the pleasures of retirement. But Astell does not declare in these lines that she intends to use her time to write poetry like Cowley or even to retire in meditation and prayer like her seventeenth-century female counterparts. She emphasizes her "Liberty" in these lines, not her devotion to God or art. Nor do these activities of earlier women describe what she *did* do with her precious solitude. But we know that she read philosophical treatises on political rights, rationalist defenses of religion, histories of the Civil War and tracts on party politics, books of economics about the effects of trade on English culture and government, and philosophical investigations of the causes of the universe, the purposes of human life, the rational basis of knowledge, and the like. And we know that she wrote her own opinions on these subjects as well, documenting the sources of her ideas with exact and copious notes. She also exercised her lively curiosity about the world around her; she read the newspapers and discussed current events with her friends; she examined the latest Grub Street pamphlets and speculated about their authorship with the *cognoscenti*; she went into society and was visited—and generally followed the intellectual debates and discoveries of literate Londoners.

Such a phenomenon would have been unthinkable earlier, not only because these issues were not commonplace subjects of speculation among private citizens, but also because women were not expected to think about them (with the exception of royal women located in the public sphere from birth), and certainly not to write, much less publish, about them. Astell was very much a product of her times in the configurations of her intellectual life, the range of her acquaintance, and the autonomous independence of her urban life—whatever the conservative Anglican cast of her mind on specific issues. In short, she had the character of an eighteenth-century woman, although her particular attitudes look backwards to the seventeenth century in which she had been raised. Thus, in the very contradictions of her life and thought, she illustrates for us important cultural shifts of the era in which she lived.

REFERENCES

1. Mary Astell and John Norris, *Letters Concerning the Love of God* (London, 1695), pp. 1-2.

2. Ibid., p. 8.

3. Ibid., p. 26.

4. Mary Astell, *A Serious Proposal To The Ladies Part II* (London, 1697), pp. 32-33.

5. Ibid, pp. 101-2.

6. Ibid., pp. 106-7.

7. Mary Astell, *A Serious Proposal To The Ladies* (London, 1694), pp. 109-110.

8. Ibid., p. 110.

9. Ibid., pp. 49-51.

10. Antoine Arnauld, *The Art of Thinking*, trans. with intro. by James Dickoff and Patricia James (Indianapolis, 1964), "Note on the Translation," p. lx.

In her excellent treatment of Astell's philosophical sources, Joan K. Kinnaird has stressed more the importance of the Cartesian influence. See "Mary Astell and the Conservative Contribution to English Feminism," *The Journal of British Studies*, XIX, No. 1 (Fall, 1979), especially pp. 59-63.

11. Régis was a minor Cartesian who, with Norris, argued that since God was the only true substance, He was the only true cause. Of the works of Nicholas Malebranche (1638-1715), Norris specifically recommended to Astell the Amsterdam edition of *Recherche de la Vérité (1674)*, the Cologne edition of *Méditations Chrétiennes* (1683) and *Traité de Morale* (Rotterdam, 1684). In the first two of these books, he directed her to the explanation of why people had not clearer notions of their own souls. Malebranche said that if they knew their own souls, people would be so ravished by the vision that they would be unable to think of anything else, not even their own bodily needs, and so would perish. Astell replied, "I am exceedingly pleas'd with M. Malbranch's Account of the Reasons why we have no Idea of our Souls, and wish I could read that ingenious Author in his own Lan-

guage, or that he spake mine." *Letters Concerning the Love of God*, p. 149. She subsequently taught herself French.

12. Antoine Arnauld, *The Art of Thinking*, trans. with intro. by James Dickoff and Patricia James, p. 7.

13. Mary Astell, *A Serious Proposal Part II*, pp. 26-7.

14. Ibid., p. 132.

15. The Port Royal Grammar and the Port Royal Logic were the first theoretical statements about language and thought which fully and sensibly embodied what Noam Chomsky calls a "Cartesian" approach to linguistics, an understanding of language as reflective of some basic human cognitive structures. Chomsky, of course, sees the Port Royal movement as a forerunner of his own brand of linguistics, and stresses that aspect of the theory which assumes a universal, underlying structure to the human mind. He is also aware of the political implications of this theory: its recognition that all minds are created more or less equal, since language use and creative capability are "universal," a "common human endowment." This premise that every human being had the same basic intellectual equipment corroborated Mary Astell's instinct about the matter, and was as welcome to her as the rules formulated at Port Royal for rigorous thought. See Noam Chomsky, *Cartesian Linguistics* (New York and London, 1966), p. 29.

16. Mary Astell, *A Serious Proposal Part II*, p. 233.

17. Mary Astell, *A Serious Proposal*, pp. 79-81.

18. George Eliot, *Middlemarch*, ed. Gordon S. Haight (Boston, 1956), pp. 6, 47.

19. See Anna Van Schurman, *The Learned Maid or, Whether a Maid may be a Scholar* (1641; translated into English 1659) and Bathsua Makin, *An Essay to Revive the Antient Education of Gentlewomen, in Religion, Manners, Arts & Tongues, with an Answer to the Objections against this Way of Education* (1673) and the anonymous *A Dialogue Concerning Women* (1691).

20. Mary Astell, *A Serious Proposal*, p. 26.

21. Mary Astell, *An Impartial Enquiry into the Causes of the Rebellion and Civil War in This Kingdom: In an Examination of Dr. Kennett's Sermon Jan. 31, 1703/4* (London, 1704), p. 42. Her position on individual liberty is much like that exposed warmly by Oliver Goldsmith's speaker, Dr. Primrose, in Chapter XIX of *The Vicar of Wakefield*:

> Now, Sir, for my own part, as I naturally hate the face of a tyrant, the farther off he is removed from me the better pleased am I. The generality of mankind also are of my way of thinking, and have unanimously created one king, whose election at once diminished the number of tyrants, and puts tyranny at the greatest distance from the greatest number of people. Now the great, who were tyrants themselves before the election of one tyrant, are naturally averse to a power raised over them, and whose weight must ever lean heaviest on the subordinate orders. It is the interest of the great, therefore, to diminish kingly power as much as possible; because, whatever they take from that is naturally restored to themselves; and all they have to do in the state is to undermine the single tyrant, by which they resume their primeval authority.

22. Mary Astell, *An Impartial Enquiry into the Causes of Rebellion and Civil War*, etc., p. 42. In addition to Clarendon's *History of the Rebellion*, published during the reign of Queen Anne, Astell recommended the following texts to her readers, to supplement and reinforce her view of the real causes of the Civil War, and her admiring portrait of that pious king, Charles I: "*Mr. Foulis's History of our pretended Saints*, Sir William Dugdale's *Short View*, Dr. Nalson, or the Declaration and Papers that Pass'd on both sides; or even their own partial Writers, in some of which, even in *Will. Lilly's Monarchy or No Monarchy*, and in *John Cook's Appeal*, the same Cook that was their Solicitor against their Sovereign, he may find as great, or greater Character of this excellent Prince, than the Doctor i.e. White Kennett gives him." Ibid., p. 37. The book by Henry Foulis (1638-1669), according

to the DNB, was thought such a masterly and compelling case for the monarch's guiltlessness, that it was "chained to desks in public places and in some churches to be read by the vulgar."

23. John Locke, *Two Treatises of Government* (London, 1690). See especially the second treatise, "An Essay Concerning the True Original, Extent and End of Civil Government," chapters IX, XL, XIX.

24. Mary Astell, *An Impartial Enquiry into the Causes of Rebellion and Civil War*, etc., p. 33.

25. Ibid., p. 8.

26. Jonathan Swift, *Gulliver's Travels*, Book II.

27. "Letter to Sir William Windham" in *Lord Bolingbroke's Works*, 4 vols. (Philadelphia, 1841), 1, 115.

28. John Locke, chapter XIX of "An Essay Concerning the True Original, Extent and End of Civil Government", in *Works*.

29. Hillel Schwartz, *Knaves, Fools, Madmen, and that Subtitle Effluvium* (Gainsville, 1978), pp. 1-30.

30. Anthony Ashley Cooper, *A Letter Concerning Enthusiasm to My Lord****** (London, 1708), p. 46.

31. Mary Astell, *Bart'lemy Fair: or, An Enquiry After Wit* (London, 1709), p. 23.

32. Ibid., p. 26.

33. Ibid., pp. 83-84.

34. Ibid., p. 60.

35. See Mary Astell, *The Christian Religion As Profess'd By A Daughter of the Church* (London, 1705), pp. 258-61.

36. This rhetorical stance is most pronounced in the 1706 Preface to *Some Reflection Upon Marriage*, originally published in 1700.

37. Ibid., 1706 preface, p. 11.

38. Mary Astell, *Some Reflections Upon Marriage* (London, 1700), p. 29.

Hawkers, Bawlers, and Mercuries: Women and the London Press in the Early Enlightenment

Margaret Hunt

Early eighteenth century London was the cultural center of a nation many enlightened Continentals considered the most innovative in Europe.[1] Here competition for control of literate culture and public opinion first reached a scale and intensity we can recognize as discernibly modern. Though there have been a number of studies of the eighteenth century London press, few scholars have made more than passing note of one very interesting phenomenon: the widespread involvement of women in the early eighteenth century publication and dissemination process.[2] These women's activities possess far more than simply antiquarian interest, for they provide us with a case-study of urban women's involvement in a form of commercial activity which was already highly capitalized by the 1720's. This essay will explore the diverse roles women played in London publishing in this period and suggest some trends that help account for their surprising prominence. A large number of the women I propose to discuss here were active in opposition publishing (i.e. the publication of politically dissident newspapers and pamphlets). Recent scholarship has attached great importance to the early eighteenth century opposition in the lineage of Western political thought.[3] The women discussed here played a part in popularizing a liberal, enlightened ideology which was to have implications for late eighteenth century revolutionary politics in America and France as well as for democratic theory, and even, it could be argued, feminism.

The spread of newspapers and book and pamphlet material in this period was remarkable. An estimate made around 1703 held

Margaret Hunt is a Ph.D. candidate at New York University and a fellow of The Institute for Research in History.

that there were at least nine newspapers being published in London with a combined circulation of about 44,000.[4] In the next twenty years both the number and combined circulation of newspapers increased at least three-fold and probably much more.[5] This trend was due in part to the rapid growth in the London population, but it was also representative of a lively interest in news, often spanning a wide spectrum of opinion and covering various classes of people, including large numbers of persons not eligible for the franchise.

The publishing industry responded with a will, though not without some inner turmoil, to its enlarged markets. The stationers' company, for centuries the guild which ordered and championed the publishing trade in all its aspects, including registering and freeing apprentices, arbitrating trade disputes, defending copyrights and disciplining refractory members, found it difficult to cope with the tremendous growth in readership and the increasingly competitive nature of the marketplace.[6] The popularity of the printed word made publishing rich ground for "parvenus", both male and female, substantial numbers of whom neither belonged to the company nor had any particular reverence for its quaint rituals. As the century went on the emergence of larger-scale businesses, erosion of paternalistic economic relations, and the sheer size of the industry as a whole was to spell the end of effective guild regulation.[7]

This was a period of growing class divisions within the trade, with few apprentices and journeymen reaching the status of self-employed artisans or masters and most condemned to lifetime dependence on a wage. As printing and publishing establishments grew larger and more impersonal in the course of the eighteenth century, both journeymen's combinations and rank-and-file challenges to the self-perpetuating hierarchy and elitist policies of the stationers' company emerged. How much women were affected by these developments remains hard to determine. We do know of women who opposed the disintegration of the live-in system of apprenticeship, a trend affecting many trades in the eighteenth century as the guilds grew weaker; but unfortunately it is difficult to be sure what these individual critics' precise motives were. The issue was more clearcut for the journeyman's associations, who were convinced that the live-out system contributed to unemployment by creating a large, mobile supply of cheap labor.[8]

While the above provides some useful background for the activities of the opposition press, the relationship between changes in the nature of the marketplace and the various ideological positions espoused by the early eighteenth century opposition (or for that matter the ruling oligarchy after 1714) remains controversial and, regrettably, beyond the scope of the present study.[9] In the early years of the century English political dissent was the province of three major groups: 1) Catholic and High Church Anglican supporters of the Stuart pretender (Jacobites), 2) tories unreconciled to the Revolution Settlement because in their view it had undermined church and king (or queen), but who were not enthusiastic about a Stuart succession, and 3) radical whigs who felt that the Revolution Settlement had not gone far enough toward limiting royal prerogative, establishing a republic, instituting a more democratic political process, and suppressing the power of the Anglican church. This latter group often appealed to the ideals of the interregnum period and was influenced by the works of Harrington and his successors.[10] After 1714, during the "moderate whig ascendancy", all these dissident groups crystallized from the government's point of view into "The Opposition". Analysis from above tended, misleadingly, to obliterate distinctions among the "upper crust" of opposition spokesmen: (Jonathan Swift as against, say, John Trenchard), but it may have been more accurate with regard to the "little" opposition whigs and tories, among whom can be found our publishers. Especially after Walpole's rise to power, these disaffected elements frequently united in opposition to the excise tax, the greed of the "financial interests" (especially the Bank of England), standing armies and government corruption.[11] To some extent regardless of party affiliation they tended to merge into the "country" or "commonwealth" tradition as described by Caroline Robbins, J.G.A. Pocock and others.[12] Strongly indebted to classical and Italian civic republicanism, the commonwealth tradition lays great stress on the role of independent, civic-minded citizens in the political process, and is fearful of anything that would interfere with this participation. Monarchical or ministerial tyranny, parliamentary corruption (bribery, sinecures, etc.), professional armies and wielding of undue influence by big financiers all tend to encourage dependence and hence civic corruption and loss of freedom.

As far as opposition publishers both male and female are concerned, however, what is perhaps more important than fitting them into a particular ideological mold is to ask the question, why did they flaunt authority as they did? Did they risk going to jail because of their political convictions or because they stood to make a profit? In the absence of much personal information on these small tradespeople this question can never be fully resolved, but neither can it be ignored. In addressing it several factors must be weighed. Opposition publishing could be quite lucrative, especially in London and especially if the piece in question had already been censured by the government or looked likely to be. At the same time, however, long term involvement in opposition publishing could be extremely risky, since the government proceeded *not* against the highly placed and powerfully connected authors of the offending books, pamphlets or newspaper articles, but against the printers, publishers and booksellers who produced and distributed them.[13]

In its efforts to control the press, the government employed spies to ferret out publishers, printers or distributors with opposition sympathies,[14] broke or confiscated presses, type, or unbound books, and arrested and jailed offending persons, often with their entire household, including apprentices, journeymen, spouses and even children.[15] It also took special steps to regulate newspapers, including levying a penny or half-penny stamp tax which could more than double their price, confiscating offending newspapers at the post office, subsidizing a government organ, paying off some newspapers to print pro-government propaganda, and outright buying control of other newspapers.[16] Considerable evidence for these activities can be found among the State Papers Domestic, our single largest source of manuscript information on the opposition press.

Women figure very prominently here. Indeed, the warrants, interrogation depositions, press-spy reports and appeals for clemency found in the State Papers Domestic provide us with some of the most detailed information we have on their professional and domestic activities, though we must look elsewhere to discover how women entered the publishing trade in the first place. For males the main mode of entry was through apprenticeship, and in 1666 we find the first formal woman apprentice in the stationers' company, Joanna Nye, daughter of a provincial clergyman.[17] This seeming evidence of liberalization is rather misleading, however. In eighteenth century London, as in previous centuries, the vast majority of women who rose to prominence in the book trade were the wives or widows of male stationers.[18] By contrast, the apprenticeship route seems not to have been very fruitful for women.

Joanna Nye, apprenticed to an engraver, was apparently never freed from her indentures and neither was a single one of the other thirty-four female apprentices bound in the latter part of the seventeenth century.[19] Did they all die or marry before their seven years were up? Or did they simply remain in their masters' households for the rest of their lives, working as household servants or semi-skilled laborers for less than journeyman's wage?

The situation of female apprentices in the eighteenth century is in some ways even more confusing, though some patterns do begin to emerge. Though we find fairly large numbers of female stationers' apprentices (300 or more in the course of the century) it is by no means clear that they were involved in printing or publishing. One frequently comes across concentrations of six or seven young women bound to a single master, often female. However, where it is possible to reconstruct the profession of the master she or he is almost always found to be either a milliner or a haberdasher, or, curiously, a mathematical instrument maker, all of these trades being occasionally included under the jurisdiction of the stationers' company.[20] This phenomenon would bear additional study for clues to the concentration of women in the needle-trades and in domestic service, but we should be wary of claiming it as proof of a broadening of opportunity for women in the book trade.

There were however two other ways women could obtain the "freedom of the stationers' company", the legal preliminary to obtaining employment as a journeyman or operating one's own business. The first, freedom by patrimony, was available only to the daughters of men who were already members of the company. The earliest case of a woman's being admitted to the company by patrimony was that of Elizabeth Latham, the daughter of George Latham, a bookseller, in 1668.[21] A more famous case was that of Tace Sowle, freed in 1695 by virtue of being the daughter of the Quaker printer Andrew Sowle. Sowle came from a line of eminent Quaker printers, her father having been arrested in the 1670's for printing "several scandalous unlicensed books" on a secret printing press. She published works like *A Vindication of Women's Preaching* (1698) and tracts by the female prophet Jane Lead, and in the 1740's became official printer for the Society of Friends.[22]

A second way of breaking into the company was for a woman to buy her way in. In the 1680's the stationers launched a campaign against small bookstalls, many of them run by women, which were undercutting the business of company members and suspected of selling pirated books. One strategy was to permit some stallholders to come into the company on paying a set fee. It is testimony to the general decline of the company, or perhaps to the low profit-margin in stall holding, that on this occasion only four women found the offer attractive enough to pay five pounds and be duly noted in the company rolls as "freed by redemption."[23]

One very important area of publishing in which women were to be found lay outside the protection of the stationers' company. Though hawking pamphlets and newspapers on the street was not an exclusively female activity, it was certainly primarily female, at least from the late seventeenth century. Exhausting, ill-paid and often dangerous, hawking was one of those marginal, semi-legal activities to which only the most desperate—the widowed, or-phaned, homeless or indigent—would have turned. Hawkers made very little money, and were often liable to charges of vagrancy or prostitution and, in some instances, imprisonment without trial.

Already by the second half of the seventeenth century the sta-tioners' company was laboring hard to suppress or control hawk-ers. In 1669, for example, the company members voted twenty shillings a quarter to the City Marshal's men to induce them to ap-prehend "Hawkers & women crying bookes near the exchange."[24] Again in 1679 they sent a deputation to the Lord Mayor to ask for the suppression of "Hawkers and Bawlers", and still again in 1684 they made applications to the Lord Chief Justice to put down hawkers because they were "the main channel through which pi-rated books [were] quickly, anonymously and *cheaply* dis-persed."[25]

Neither the actions of the stationers' company nor the many or-dinances passed against hawkers did away with them; indeed they grew, if anything, more numerous with the growth of the newspa-per trade, and whereas some stuck to "legal" material, others could always be found hawking unlicensed newspapers, incendiary pam-phlets or pornographic broadsides. Some, at least, made a habit of selling illegal material, either because the remuneration was higher or because they had no other options. Thus in 1744

. . . Ann Mahony, otherwise Irish Nan, was committed to Clerkenwell-Bridewell, for three months to hard labor . . . for selling unstamp'd News-Papers. This is the seventh Time of her being committed for Offenses of the like nature.[26]

Hawkers were at the bottom of the hierarchy of the trade, but they were nevertheless an important link in the newspaper and pamphlet dissemination process.[27]

An area about which relatively little is known, but of primary importance for the present study, is the occupation of mercury. In the mid-seventeenth century mercuries were, apparently, simply hawkers of pamphlets, "the mercuries that cry about books;" and there is some indication that by 1666, at least, they were associated specifically with prohibited pamphlets.[28] By the 1680's, however, with the proliferation of newspapers, "mercury" came to be a gender-specific term for a women who bought newspapers wholesale from the printer and then either dispersed them to hawkers or sold them retail out of a shop. According to a recent study of the publishing trade, "the bulk of" London newspapers in the early eighteenth century were distributed through this route.[29]

John Dunton, a contemporary, supplies additional evidence that "mercuries" (in the sense of retailers and wholesalers of newspapers from a shop) were always women. In his *Life and Errors* (1705) he lists what he calls

> . . . the honest (mercurial) women, Mrs. Baldwin, Mrs. Nutt, Mrs. Curtis, Mrs. Mallett, Mrs. Croom, Mrs. Grover, Mrs. Barnes, Mrs. Winter, Mrs. Taylor, . . .[30]

In this regard it is also useful to note the lists of names and professions of persons arrested for libel in the 1720's and 30's, where the descriptive term "mercury" is used exclusively for women.[31] There were undoubtedly some male booksellers who also handled newspapers, but they seem not to have been as well known nor to have had such substantial businesses as the women in Dunton's list or other mercuries for whom evidence has survived. Mercuries, especially if they were the wives or widows of printers or booksellers, were in a position to make valuable contacts and develop a keen sense of the public taste in news. This, coupled with the fact that some mercuries appear to have been realizing considerable profit, makes it perhaps not so surprising that some went beyond distribution into the actual production of newspapers. In 1702, for example, the first English daily newspaper, *The Daily Courant*, was started by Elizabeth Mallett, one of Dunton's "mercurial" women.[32] Two years later Ann Baldwin, radical whig and widow of the printer, Richard Baldwin, used her contacts among the French Huguenot refugee population of London to publish a French language newspaper which was distributed both in London and abroad.[33]

Ann Baldwin also became involved in one of those curious practices of the period, "newspaper wars"; in this case she contrived to publish spurious editions of a periodical called *The Medley*, after its editor had taken to a new publisher.[34] Between 1709 and 1710 she went into partnership with the writer and dramatist Mary de la Rivière Manley to publish a women's journal called the *Female Tatler*. One of the earliest women's magazines, and probably the first to have both a woman editor and a woman publisher, the *Female Tatler* was also one of the first women's magazines to get into trouble with the law. In 1709 both Baldwin and Manley were indicted by the Grand Jury of Middlesex, which declared that:

> A Great Number of printed Papers are continually dispersed under the name of the Female Tatler sold by A. Baldwin . . . [which] reflect on and scandalously abuse several persons of honour and quality, many of the magistrates and [an] abundance of citizens and all sorts of people . . . which practice we conceive to be a great nuisance. We therefore humbly hope this honourable court will take effectual care to prevent these abuses as their wisdom shall see fit.[35]

As the above passage suggests and a sampling of the *Female Tatler* tends to confirm, the effort to suppress the newspaper was not due to any feminist sentiment expressed or implied in its pages but rather to the paper's disrespectful attitude toward persons "of quality". Probably the fact that Ann Baldwin was already a well-known publisher of radical whig material was also a contributing factor.[36]

It was in the still underdeveloped newspaper trade, as opposed to other branches of the printing and publishing industry, that women were to be found in the largest numbers. At certain moments in the early part of the century they may actually have predominated in this trade (and certainly in the distribution part of it) relative to men. Between 1701 and 1740, for example, more than thirty newspapers show a woman as either publisher, printer, editor or major distributor.[37] Ann Baldwin and Elizabeth Mallett between them appear to have controlled five out of seven of the new serial ventures launched in the year 1701.[38] Ann Dodd, between 1711 and 1735, launched or helped to launch at least six separate periodicals, some in partnership with Elizabeth Nutt.[39]

It is rare, however, to find women who confined themselves solely to newspapers; indeed, given the precarious nature of the genre, the tremendous competition and the ever-present possibility, for the opposition journals at least, of governmental harassment, such a narrow focus would have been financially disastrous. We find women listed frequently on books or pamphlets of the period as printers, publishers or booksellers, the usual practice at the time being to indicate all three on the title page or on book advertisements. We also find women as members of wholesaling and printing congers, groups organized cooperatively to safeguard jointly owned copyrights and launch more ambitious publishing ventures than a single individual could safely handle.[40] In one of the earliest known congers, Rebecca Bonwicke was apparently the leading figure.[41] The congers about which we know the most are free associations of eight or more of the largest and most successful members of the trade, people who in combination could wield considerable influence. Congers are still a relatively unknown aspect of the trade and we know little about humbler sorts of congers, though title-pages alone give us plenty of evidence of partnerships or group activities both short and long term. Interestingly, we find a number of largely-female combinations, as in the case of an ambitious 1735 project, *Annotations on the Holy Bible*, whose participants include J. Read (sex unknown), Elizabeth Nutt, Ruth Charlton, M. Cooke (sex unknown, possibly Mary Cooke) and Ann Dodd.[42] This combination is especially interesting because Ann Dodd, Elizabeth Nutt and Ruth Charlton were major newspaper distributors who in modern times would be likely to view themselves as competitors.

Though there is no clear evidence of a newspaper-owning conger made up predominantly of mercuries, there is a strong likelihood, based on advertisements in leading opposition journals, that Dodd and Nutt owned controlling interests in one or more of these newspapers in the 1720's and '30's. For these two women, and probably other mercuries as well, their close involvement with newspapers and newspaper distribution was probably a decisive factor in the evolution of their bookselling businesses. Their connections allowed them easy and cheap access to advertising space in major periodicals with circulations of tens of thousands of copies in some cases. It is not uncommon to find one or two mercuries monopolizing up to three-quarters of the advertising space for months at a time in a major newspaper.[43] Indeed in the decade and a half between 1720 and 1735 the mercuries actually appear for a short time to have gained a competitive edge over the majority of the male booksellers, who either did not catch on as readily to the benefits of newspaper advertising or could not place ads so easily and cheaply.[44] There are few more ubiquitous names on the title pages of books of this period than those of Dodd and Nutt.

Were women, as the State Papers Domestic seem to suggest, disproportionately likely to be involved in radical, illegal or opposition publishing as opposed to "orthodox" publishing? Though one can only conjecture, it seems quite possible that the semi-clandestine, insecure, but also highly charged atmosphere in which opposition pieces were produced offered a strong inducement for all members of a family or household, including women and girls, to become more directly involved in all aspects of production.[45] Certainly for economic reasons, it would have been advantageous for the master's wife to be able to take over supervision of the business if her husband was jailed or had to get out of town quickly, as not infrequently happened. At any rate by the 1730's few would have thought it strange when the secretary of state's assault on an offending issue of Francklin's *The Craftsman* began with a warrant naming three mercuries. The original reads as follows:

> These are in His Majesty's name to authorise and require you (taking a constable to your assistance) to make strict and diligent search for Ann Dodd, Eliz. Nutt and Ann Smith of whom you shall have notice and them or any of them having found you are to seise and apprehend for publishing two false, Scandalous and Seditious libels, the one entitled The Country Journal or The Craftsman by Caleb D'Anvers . . . [issue of] Saturday, January 2, 1730 No. 235, and the other . . . [same paper, issue of] Saturday January 9, 1730 No. 236 and to bring them or any of them together with their papers in safe custody before me to be examined concerning the premises and to be further dealt with according to the law. . . .[46]

Ann Dodd as early as 1721 was a major distributor of at least one important opposition paper, the *London Journal*. For one extended edition, of which 10,000 copies were printed, she took in 2,700, or more than a quarter of the copies of this nationally distributed paper.[47] Her name appears frequently in State Papers, in newspaper advertisements, and on book title pages, and consequently we can reconstruct her career with more than usual detail. Something of her *modus operandi* comes out in a police interrogation in 1721 of one William Hewitt in connection with the *London Journal* No. 107 of 12 August of that year. Hewitt, who is "living at Mr. Dodds at ye Sign of the Peacock, Temple Bar," reports having

> served the said Mr. Dodd about a year and a half, the said Mr. Dodd's wife being a Retailler of News Papers & Pamphlets commonly called a Mercury. The Examinant is always sent to the publisher of such Papers to such quantity thereof as Mrs. Dodd had occasion for . . .[48]

The Dodd ménage had also been involved the year before in another illegal enterprise, this time the distribution of an anti-trinitarian tract. The book was *A Sober Reply to Mr. Higgs' Merry Arguments, from the Light of Nature, for the Tritheistick Doctrine of the Trinity* (1720), published by Elizabeth Smith, who was frequently in partnership with Ann Dodd, Elizabeth Nutt or her daughters, Ruth Charlton, and other producers of "offending material."[49] The book inspired the appointment of a committee of inquiry of ninety-nine members of the House of Lords, and the following statement from a member of the committee, the Archbishop of York:

> . . . the whole book is a mixture of the most scandalous Blasphemy, Profaneness, and Obscenity; and does in a most daring, impious, Manner, ridicule the doctrine of the Trinity and all Revealed Religion.[50]

Elizabeth Smith on being taken into custody announced that her name had been placed on the book without her knowledge and she was released, though the author and printers of the book were directed to be prosecuted and the book condemned to be burnt on 16 February 1720. Two days later, however, the authorities were horrified to discover that a great number of Books, the same with that ordered to be burnt Yesterday were dispersed and publicly sold in West-minister Hall and other places. . . .[51]

One John Stagg, bookseller, then testified "that Mr. Dodd's man . . . left him at his shop . . . a dozen of these books." Dodd, on being sent for, said that he had not known the books had been "censured,"[52] At this point the case was inexplicably dropped, perhaps due to fatigue on the part of the authorities.

Publishing people who were frequently in trouble with the law possessed well-developed strategies designed to protect themselves and their associates from harassment or prosecution. A clean sweep in August 1728 of twenty-four persons connected with the printing, publishing and disseminating of the Jacobite *Mist's Weekly Journal* of 24 August 1728 netted apprentices, journey-men, servants, mercuries and a small boy, Nathaniel Mist's ne-phew.[53] Among those taken were Elizabeth Smith, Alice Nutt (the daughter of Elizabeth Nutt), Ann Neville, and one William Howard, listed as "Dod's Man" (Ann Dodd was by this time wid-owed). Also taken was Dr. Gaylard, who had been in trouble be-fore and who, this time, decided to dispense with "trade solidarity" and inform on his associates in order "to prevent ye speedy ruin which must otherwise immediately fall upon ye family of your honour's unhappy humble servant."[54]

The others who were taken were by no means as forthcoming, either then or less than a month later, when a number of them were pulled back into custody for producing and distributing the *Mist's* of September 7 and 14, 1728. The bookseller John Wilford indi-cated that he did not know the author of the libel and stated that:

the said libel was published in ye usuall manner by sending it out [to] ye mercurys as they are called who make a Trade of selling Newspapers and Pamphlets and retailing them out to the hawkers and that as they were not delivered by him he cannot give any account of the particular persons.[55]

Ann Neville was no more illuminating even though she had been caught with nineteen quires of the libel on her person. Ac-cording to the interrogation report:

She [says] she knows not where they came & ye man who brought them was a stranger to her . . . she is but a servant of Eliz. Nutt and did not do this on her own account . . .

However, she also stated, in an effort to vindicate the Nutts, that:

. . . she had not any particular orders relating to this individual paper from her mistress, her said mistress being then in custody.[56]

Sarah Nutt, who was minding the shop while her mother was in prison, was also brought in for questioning but said she had "resolved not to take in any more Mist's Journals."[57] In the meantime Ann Dodd, who had evidently been named in one of the *Mist's Journal* warrants but who was conveniently out of town, wrote the following petition, the original of which is found among the State Papers Domestic, to "his Grace the Duke of Newcastle," stating that:

. . . your Grace's Petitioner hath been long confined to her chamber in the Country, tho' a violent & dangerous Indisposition, & still continues in a very ill State of Health.

Yet in obedience to your Grace's Warrant issued agt Her, She is notwithstanding her Weak Condition, willing to come to Town, hoping upon a Surrender of her Person, your Grace will be pleased to admit her to Bail, without any confinement, for should she be imprisoned her life w'd be inevitably endangered.

This act of your Grace's Clemency she most humbly implores, and as in duty bound will ever Pray & c.

Ann Dodd[58]

The *Mist's Weekly Journal* arrests of 1728, which are in no way unique except perhaps for the large number of people initially taken, demonstrate several important characteristics of the opposition press. As mentioned above, one was the loyalty of most booksellers, printers, etc. to their associates (and employers) in the trade. We repeatedly find them pleading ignorance of the other

people involved, the original source of the offending pieces, and
so on. Sometimes the stories border on the ludicrous, as in the
case of the bookseller who claimed that "a masked woman" left
the libelous books at his shop.[59] People in the trade must often
have been called upon to put up bail for each other or to provide
sureties. In the *Mist's* case, for example, Alice Nutt was bailed out
with twenty pounds, probably by her sister.[60] We also have evidence of printers' and publishers' taking up collections for associates who had lost their stock through fire, collections to which
women generously contributed,[61] and there is a manuscript from
1743 in the British Library from the printer Daniel Pratt, whose
master had been a business associate of the mercury Elizabeth
Smith, stating that the printers of unstamped papers "keep up a
Bank, to maintain such of their Hawkers that are or may be putt in
prison for selling the same."[62] It is difficult to know whether to
account for these practices by reference to guild tradition, vertical
trade solidarity, or shared political commitment, but what is interesting is that women apparently participated fully both in the sacri-
fices and the benefits.

These episodes also illustrate the tendency, mentioned above,
for family members to succeed to the running of the business while
the main proprietor was in jail. We find numerous instances of
this in both the seventeenth and eighteenth centuries, frequently involving wives, sisters or daughters. Thus Margaret Haines printed
the *Craftsman* when her brother Henry was in King's Bench Prison,[63] while various Nutt daughters seem to be almost constantly
filling in for their mother Elizabeth during her numerous sojourns
in prison.[64] In the late seventeenth century Benjamin Harris' wife
ran his business when he was in jail, and is said to have "stood by
him to defend her husband against the mob" when he was put in
the pillory for publishing seditious material.[65]

Evident too in the *Mist's* case is the degree to which political
radicalism, religious heterodoxy and involvement in opposition
publishing were passed from generation to generation. Certainly
this was true of the Quaker publishers, the Sowles, as well as the
Nutts and another family, the Mears or Meeres, with whom the
Nutts intermarried. Hugh Mear published the *Historical Register*
of the Sun Fire Insurance Office from at least 1716, in which appeared the first parliamentary debates, and from 1722 the *British
Journal*, famous for the publication of one of the major radical
whig tracts of the century, *Cato's Letters*. The Meeres lived from

1722 (though perhaps there is no personal connection here) in the house of the ill-fated republican, Algernon Sidney, who had been beheaded in 1683 for alleged involvement in the Rye House Plot.[66] Upon Meere's death his widow Cassandra took over the business and we find her listed as C. Meere of the Old Bailey "said to be a high flyer" (i.e., part of the opposition) in Samuel Negus' famous, if occasionally unreliable, 1724 list of London printers with their political affiliations.[67] In the twenties, their daughter Elizabeth married Richard Nutt, thus linking the two families, and from then on, successive generations of Nutts and Meeres were in trouble for most of the rest of the century. The names of Sarah, Catherine and Alice Nutt, probably Elizabeth Nutt's daughters,[68] all appear regularly on arrest warrants and other judicial records. In 1734, for example, Alice Nutt, listed in the records as "Spinster," was held over at the King's Bench for publishing or selling no less than five "seditious libels."[69] Sarah Nutt had bail set for her at 200 pounds in 1743/4 for an unspecified offense.[70] In 1735 Sarah sold the radical whig classic, *The Religious and Moral Conduct of Mathew Tyndale.*[71] Richard Nutt was elected to the anti-Walpole Common Council in 1736, and in 1742, after a spat with the oligarchical leadership of the stationers' company, wrote and published a pamphlet entitled *The Pomp and Grandeur of the Master, Wardens and Assistants and their Relations and Dependents [who] have long stood upon the Miseries of the Freemen.* Using a type of language usually reserved for attacks on the whig ministry, the pamphlet called for upholding the rights and freedoms of "poor printers and bookbinders." Clearly these publishers were capable of applying the country rhetoric to their own distinctive trade problems as well as to the larger political polity. In 1754 Richard Nutt was fined 500 pounds, and sentenced to stand in the pillory and to two years imprisonment for having "attributed the miserable state of the country to the revolution settlement."[72] He was also proceeded against for his role in publishing the *London Evening Post*, the *Universal Spectator* and the *Daily Post*,[73] John Mears (probably his cousin) took over part of the business in the late 1730's and was imprisoned, fined or put in the pillory several times in the 1740's and 1750's. In 1745 he was accused of having "barely concealed Jacobite tendencies,"[74] but I have not been able to discover additional evidence for this, and it may simply have been another effort by the government to discredit its opposition in the face of the '45 uprising.

It is not clear whether William Mears, who published the notorious free-thinker and materialist Alberto Radicati di Passerano's *Philosophical Dissertation on Death* (1732) was related to this family or not; the available sources seem to indicate he is not.[75] Of some interest, however, is the fact in that same year Eizabeth Nutt, Ann Dodd and Elizabeth Cooke, in partnership, published Radicati's *History of the Abdication of Victor Amadeus II, Late King of Sardinia.*[76] Radicati was residing at London at that time, having been banished from his native country, and he was to suffer considerable persecution from the English authorities.[77]

In 1761 John Mears senior died, and his son, also John, inherited the business and the running of the *London Evening Post.* Only three years later he was fined 100 pounds for publishing an article written by John Almon, bookseller and friend of John Wilkes, in which a peer was mentioned by name. The *London Evening Post* was subsequently in the thick of the Wilkes controversy. Here we can see a continuous heritage of urban radicalism stretching back at least sixty years through opposition publishing families.[78]

The very pervasiveness of the family connection tells much about the trade, however. The necessity that a woman be born into a publishing family or that she marry a man in the trade, or both, before she had even a small chance of serious involvement in the book or newspaper business severely limited most women's access to the trade. Familial connections were important for men too, but by no means to this degree. Virtually without exception we can find no women who rose to prominence except through the medium of a man, either father, brother, or husband, though it must also be stated that most of the women developed very distinct types of businesses, frequently in a different branch of the trade from their male relatives.

It would be a mistake to claim these people definitely for either the "radical whig" or "tory" camp: like many urban radicals of the first half of the eighteenth century they were eclectics who moved with surprisingly little effort back and forth between the two. Ann Baldwin at the very beginning of the century would have called herself a "true whig," yet much of the material she published differs little from that of Ann Dodd or Elizabeth Nutt, both of whom distributed the Jacobite *Mist's Weekly Journal* in the 1720's.[79] Most likely some of these later women flirted with Jacobitism, but much of what they published would have been totally unacceptable

in the "high tory" camp because of its anti-monarchical or reli-
giously heterodox tone. As publishers they were at least as attracted by radical whig or commonwealth ideas, in particular
republicanism. In 1733 Elizabeth Nutt and H. Curll (actually Edmund Curll) published Matthew Tindal's *Essay on the Inconsistency of Absolute Submission to Princes*,[80] while in 1743 "Mrs.
Cooke of the Royal Exchange" (probably Elizabeth Cooke) and
Ann Dodd published a tract attributed to Cromwell.[81] In 1719
Ann Dodd and J. Roberts launched a short-lived periodical called
the *Old Whig*, which after a lapse of sixteen years Roberts revived
as The *Old Whig or the Consistent Protestant*.[82]

Certainly these women display no high-church sympathies.
Rather, they can be seen distributing anti-trinitarian tracts, scurri-
lous and often pornographic attacks on Catholic clerics,[83] and
even works by the pantheistic materialist Alberto Radicati, as well
as those of the homegrown anticleric and champion of "natural religion", John ("Orator") Henley.[84] Few would have gone quite so
far as Jacob Ilive, printer, type-founder and author, who in 1733,
"pursuant to the will of his mother," Jane Ilive, a printer's widow
who is said to have "shared his religious views," wrote and published a book against eternal punishment, followed shortly there-
after by A *Dialogue . . . wherein it is proved that the Miracles
said to be wrought by Moses were artificial acts only* and other
tracts, which landed him in Clerkenwell Prison at hard labor.[85]
The mercury women of the twenties and thirties would not have
been particularly shocked, though they might have thought Ilive a
little unwise.

They were, after all, rather practical people with families to
support and they had a quite well-developed sense of self-preserva-
tion, as we can see from yet another appeal by Ann Dodd, written
this time from prison. Dated May 26, 1731, it is worth reproduc-
ing in its entirety:

May it Please your Grace:

I most humbly beg leave to trouble your grace with these
few lines. I have been left an afflicted widow with a Large
Young family some years, whose only support has been sell-
ing news papers; which, with as much pains as my own Ill
State of Health would admit of, has by the Assistance of
Heaven, just enabled me to Feed my Self and helpless Chil-

dren. I need not Acquaint your Grace that this Business sometimes Compells me to sell Papers that give Offence, but I must beg Leave to Declare Sincerely 'tis Greatly Against my Inclination when they are so, and that what papers I sell in Just Praise of Our Happy Government far exceeds the Others in Number. Hard case! that I must either Offend where I am shure I would not, or else Starve my Poor Babes. I am to be Tried next Tuesday for selling a Craftsman, a paper that I neither Read nor Understand. I Beseech you let my Children plead with your Grace to put a stop to the Proceedings, which I Trust a Line, or two, from your Grace's Hand, would effectually do. Your Grace's Known Character is, To Do Good, and to shew Mercy, and where can that goodness and that Mercy, be Better shewn, than by helping the Fatherless and Widow[.] [I]f I have offended, tis an ignorant offence and as the Distressed have always the surest Title to your Grace's Protection; mine will in the strongest Terms plead for

> may it please your grace
> Your Graces
> most obedient and most humble servant
>
> Ann Dodd.[86]

Whether or not this appeal got Ann Dodd out of prison and reunited with her Poor Babes is unknown, but she was back in action again, seemingly undeterred, just one year later when, along with Elizabeth Nutt and Edmund Curll, she published *The Pleasures and Mysteries of the Marriage Bed Modestly Unveiled; An Instructive Poem for Young Brides.*[87] Indeed a well-developed libertine aspect can be noted in a number of these women's publications, a characteristic they shared with many of the "enlightened" across the channel.

Ann Dodd followed this up in 1736 with a translation of Cordonnier de Saint-Hyacinthe's *History of Prince Titi*, a thinly-disguised satire on royal families.[88] Saint-Hyacinthe (1684-1746) was a deist, republican and expatriate Frenchman who had strong ties both with radical freethinkers in the Netherlands and with "commonwealthmen" in England, where he eventually settled. Like Radicati, his career allows us to glimpse the "internationalist" aspect of radical whig ideology: its profound hostility towards absolutism (especially of the French variety) and the Catholic church, and its preference for republican, rather than oligarchical or monarchical government.[89] It is no coincidence that Ann Dodd, Elizabeth Nutt and others of their circle were publishing works by such people, or that both Radicati and Saint-Hyacinthe found a temporary haven among the radical whigs of the opposition.

Women printers and publishers, in particular the mercuries, also played an active role in at least one important propaganda campaign whose impetus came largely from the book trade itself, and especially from its opposition wing—the campaign for greater freedom of the press. Viewed perhaps too frequently by historians as an abstract "right," freedom of the press was a bread-and-butter issue as well as an ideological one for the mercury women whose major income derived from newspaper sales, and who probably owned shares in opposition papers. One of the major "free press" controversies of the century centered around the publication of parliamentary debates, and more generally around the right of newspapers to report upon the inner workings of government and foreign policy. In an era in which traditional preoccupations with religion and the hereafter seemed everywhere to be giving way to concern with parliamentary politics, international affairs, and the economy, purveyors of the news were responding to an ever-growing demand. The necessity to court mass support was becoming, perhaps for the first time in British history, almost universally recognized as an integral part of the political process. Predictably, it was the opposition press which pressed hardest on the issue of press freedom, in part no doubt because parliamentary reports and diplomatic correspondence sold papers, but in part also because to that wing of the opposition influenced by republican or proto-democratic ideas (what we have come to call the "commonwealth tradition"), it was axiomatic that "the people" had a right to know what the government was doing. And this was a period when "the people" was being increasingly broadly defined, in political theory if not the actual exercise of the elective franchise.

Perusing the major "free press" tracts of the first half of the eighteenth century, we find that a surprising percentage were published by mercury women, or by their close business associates. In a recent series of six modern reprints of major works written on freedom of the press between 1712 and 1730, two were originally published by Ann Baldwin, one by Rebecca and James Bonwicke, one each by J. Roberts and J. Wilford (both frequently in partnership with Ann Dodd), and one by Elizabeth and Richard Nutt.[90]

In the 1740s yet another major series of pieces on the freedom of the press appeared in Jane Morgan's *Old England, or the Constitutional Journal*, a paper she apparently published out of the house of her widowed sister, Mary Cooper, and for which both were brought in for questioning in 1744.[91] In 1748 Mary Cooper republished the pieces on freedom of the press as a collection entitled *The Importance of Liberty of the Press: Shewing how Greatly it Affects all Degrees of Men, as well with Respect to Religion as Private Property and National Liberty*.[92] It is a fine piece of "commonwealth" writing, staunchly opposed to "hereditary kingship" and divine right theory because tyrants (Charles I and II are mentioned by name) always endeavor to:

> extinguish the natural light of Understanding in the Subject, least it should be exercised in enquiring upon what Ground or Authority one sett of men claim to tyrannize over another . . . and least they [the subjects] should learn from History and the Rise, Progress and Growth of Power, which their persecutors pretend to derive from Heaven. . . .[93]

For this author, "the Benefit of the [free] Press is a constant Bulwark against the otherwise certain Approaches of Tyranny,"[94] and this is demonstrated by the histories of Greece and Italy, "where Liberty and Learning have gone hand in hand, have together flourished and sunk by equal Degrees."[95] It is the "spirit of the nation"[96] that gives force to law and checks its abuses, but this same spirit which "was so strong in Favour of Liberty" during the Revolution of '88–'89[97] has of late been perverted and rendered slavish and dependent by "Excise Laws, the Establishment of Funds [i.e., the public debt], standing Armies and new-created Places."[98]

The writer speaks warmly of the "glorious" and tragic death of the republican Algernon Sidney, who was one of the "greatest Ornaments of our Country . . . ,"[99] and maintains that

> . . . to hinder the People from complaining, who upon the Principles of the Revolution have a right to more than complaining, have a Right to Redress, nay, and to redress themselves, [is] contrary to the Spirit and Sense of the Revolution.[100]

The author, whoever he or she may be, favors tolerance for non-conformists, and is especially disturbed at the prospect of ecclesiastical censorship and too strict adherence to religious dogma, for:

> . . . when religious Tenets are laid down in so positive a Manner, . . . the next Step is a pretended or real concern for Brethren walking in Darkness . . . to which succeeds that Christian compassion of Saving Men's Souls by Inquisitions, and all that Tyranny of the Church of *Rome*, so much abhorred in this Country at present.[101]

The Importance of Liberty of the Press is by no means an extremist document; it makes a deliberate effort to sound moderate and high-minded, purports to be written by a member of the Church of England, and contains several obligatory-sounding references to the virtues of the present ministry.[102] Nonetheless, with its unmistakable approval of popular sovereignty, its oblique references to the Italian and ancient Greek republics, its concern that civic morality is being undermined by standing armies and placemen, its glowing references to the commonwealth martyr Algernon Sidney, and its hostility towards religious dogma and Catholicism in particular, this "free-press" tract demonstrates the continued currency of commonwealth ideas in the opposition, and the central place of that ideology in the ferment of ideas we call the age of reason. This is, among other things, the ideological stream which led to Mary Wollstonecraft's *Vindication of the Rights of Women*. It is no coincidence that Wollstonecraft's attack on Rousseau's *Émile* is based upon the old commonwealth identification of dependency with moral corruption and loss of liberty. She even explicitly compares the moral position of women with the moral position of soldiers in a standing army.[103]

London mercuries played a central role in distributing propaganda that directly or by implication called for greater parliamentary accountability and a broader political role for the free-born citizen—in some later formulations even an expanded franchise. Yet there is no evidence that the democratizing tendencies implicit in some (though not all) aspects of commonwealth thought had the least impact on these women's own prospects for formal political participation. There were definitely limitations on how far a woman could go in the trade without the privilege of buying into the company livery or holding office in the stationers' company. James Roberts, four times master of the stationers' company (1729-31), is only one of several business associates of Ann Dodd, Elizabeth Nutt and other mercuries who subsequently rose to high office in the stationers' company, something the women could not aspire to.[104] We do not know to what extent this exclusion hindered women's conduct of their businesses, but the effect was surely not negligible. Whether or not one could hold office in one's trade company had a still larger political significance, moreover, for it was mainly through this route that the male Londoner of ambition but relatively humble origins moved into municipal, county and even national office, both elective and appointive.[105] While there were no doubt other factors militating against female involvement in formal politics in the early eighteenth century, it is interesting that for women in the book trade the door to the corridors of power slammed shut most emphatically in their own trade association.

There is deep irony in the fact that these women, as much as their confrères (indeed more so, because of their distinctive association with the distribution of newspapers) were on the front line of the opposition. Almost all the mercuries knew what it was to be in prison and to have to raise bail money or sureties. Several had a half-dozen or more warrants out for them in their time, and most had undergone repeated police interrogations and/or confiscation of their stock. And what precisely were they distributing? Jacobite newspapers in some cases, it is true. But they were also printing, publishing and selling tracts that were republican, in favour of free access to information on the activities of government, and opposed to organized religion—in short, literature that was very much a part of that secular and democratizing (if not democratic) impulse that we know as the Enlightenment. It is an indication of the limitations of that enlightened ideology that even when the very currency of these ideas owed so much to the activities of a group of newspaper women, it did not extend its analysis or its rhetoric to include them in any substantial way. Yet one could argue too that there is a sense in which these women transcended those limitations in the way they lived and worked from day to day. Like some of their more famous contemporaries both in England and the Continent, they were disrespectful of ecclesiastical and political authority, intrigued by heresy (especially if it would sell) and willing to sacrifice economic security and sometimes personal freedom to promulgate new ideas. They were independent women playing distinct roles in their trade, and as much as any group of women in the eighteenth century they could see themselves as having a political impact, not, of course, directly through the franchise (denied to some of their male associates as well) but through the avenue of molding public opinion.

There were other changes at work, however, which before the eighteenth century was over would mean the virtual disappearance of urban women from the more remunerative and influential branches of the book and newspaper trades, and their concentration in hawking, prostitution, domestic service, the needle trades, or "middle class" domesticity, depending on their luck or class. The mercuries who had so effectively exploited the still-young newspaper industry and gone on to substantial involvement in book and pamphlet publishing in the early eighteenth century were gradually, by a complex process that we still do not fully understand, replaced by men. By 1750 they were almost gone.

A hundred years later the London landscape had changed totally. We can find almost no women in the printing, publishing and bookselling trade directories, and those few who do appear are small retail shop holders who do not publish and appear isolated from the rest of the trade.[106] The various terms for sellers of newspapers in use in the first half of the eighteenth century, all of them non-gender-specific or female-specific ("news-sellers," "news-carriers," "mercuries"), have given way almost exclusively to the term "newspaper men."[107] Nor had women found a sympathetic hearing in the fledgling journeyman's associations which, as is so many other trades, saw women workers as a threat to their own employment.[108]

So the mercury women were part of a temporary phenomenon in which a "peripheral" sales and distribution task that may traditionally have been assigned to women in the family economy of a printing or publishing establishment suddenly took off in importance under the forces of economic expansion and relative political liberalization, allowing some women to play a much more than peripheral role in their trade. The expanding market economy in which these women enjoyed fleeting prominence was, at an only slightly later stage in its development, to cut them off from all but the most narrow kinds of economic activity. It is, however, for future scholarship to explore the precise interplay of social, economic and ideological forces that led to women's virtual disappearance from positions of authority within the printing and publishing industry. For our present purposes the mercury women and other women of the London press continue to represent one of the few groups of women in the eighteenth century to play a discernible, indeed a distinctive role in furthering enlightenment, both in the way they appear to have conducted their lives and in the newspapers, pamphlets and books that were their livelihood.

REFERENCES

1. I would like to thank the following persons who gave generously of their time in commenting upon this paper: Louise Connell, Margaret Jacob, Mary Nolan, Susan Yohn, James Jacob, Barbara Balliet, Howard Negrin, Darline Levy, Ruth Graham, Phyllis Mack, Ruth Perry, Eleanor Riemer and the Intellectual History Seminar of the Institute for Research in History. The responsibility for any errors that may have occurred is mine alone.

2. For background on the opposition press see the old but still useful Laurence Hanson, *The Government and the Press, 1695-1763* (Oxford, 1936) and Charles Ripley Gillett, *Burned Books; Neglected Chapters in British History and Literature* (New York, 1932). A more recent study is Bertrand Goldgar, *Walpole and the Wits* (Lincoln, 1976). The only study which gives thorough attention to the activities of women in the trade is Michael Harris, "The London Newspaper Press ca. 1725-1746" (Unpublished PhD thesis, University of London, 1973).

3. J. G. A. Pocock, "Post-Puritan England and the Problem of the Enlightenment", in Perez Zagorin, ed., *Culture and Politics from Puritanism to the Enlightenment* (Berkeley, 1980), pp. 91 ff.

4. James R. Sutherland, "The Circulation of Newspapers and Literary Periodicals, 1700-30," *The Library*, Fourth Series, Vol. XV, 1935, pp. 111-12.

5. Ibid., p. 116.

6. Peter Burke, *Popular Culture in Early Modern Europe* (London, 1979), p. 251, puts male literacy in England at 60% in the second half of the eighteenth century and mentions that it had increased markedly since 1650. Literacy would have been lower among women and people living outside large cities. See also Michael Harris' extremely useful chapter, "The Structure, Ownership and Control of the Press, 1620-1780", in George Boyce, James Curran and Pauline Wingate, eds. *Newspaper History from the Seventeenth Century to the Present Day* (London, 1978), pp. 82-97, for a description of the eighteenth century market in books and newspapers.

7. Cyprian Blagden, *The Stationers' Company: A History, 1403-1959* (Cambridge, 1960), pp. 175-77.

8. For challenges to the Stationers' Company oligarchy see Richard Nutt, *The Pomp and Grandeur of the Master, Wardens and Assistants [of the Stationers' Company] and their Relations and Dependents [who] have long stood upon the Miseries of the Freemen* (London, 1742); also the career of James Ilive described in the *Dictionary of National Biography* (hereafter *DNB*) and in Edward Rowe Mores, *A Dissertation upon English Typographical Founders and Founderies* . . . [etc.] (Oxford, 1961) pp. 60-62, 121-22. For a woman's opposition to the "live-out" system see Eleanor James, *Advice to all Printers* (London, 1720), and for journeyman opposition see Ellic Howe and Harold E. Waite, *London Society of Compositors* . . . *a Centenary History* (London, 1948), pp. 73-4.

9. For a recent contribution to the debate see J. G. A. Pocock, "Radical Criticisms of the Whig Order in the Age between Revolutions", in Margaret Jacob and James Jacob, eds., *The Origins of Anglo-American Radicalism* (London, 1984), pp. 33-57.

10. For the make-up of the opposition see especially J.G.A. Pocock, *The Machiavellian Moment: Florentine Political Thought and the Atlantic Republic Tradition* (Princeton, 1975), pp. 468-86; also W. A. Speck, *Stability and Strife: England 1714-1760* (London, 1977), pp. 219-38, and Geoffrey Holmes, *British Politics in the Age of Anne* (London, 1967), pp. 116-47.

11. See in its entirety Paul Langford, *The Excise Crisis: Society and Politics in the Age of Walpole* (Oxford, 1975).

12. Caroline Robbins, *The Eighteenth-Century Commonwealthmen: Studies in the Transmission, Development and Circumstances of English Liberal Thought* [etc.] . . . (Cambridge, Mass., 1959); Pocock, *The Machiavellian Moment* . . . Chapters 10-15.

13. Donald Thomas, "Press Prosecutions of the Eighteenth and Nineteenth Centuries," *The Library*, Fifth Series, Vol. XXXII, No. 4, 1977, p. 316.

14. One of the most famous of these is the notorious Edmund Curll; also interesting in this regard is Samuel Negus' 1724 list of London printers complete with their political affiliations, which he compiled for the benefit of the government. The list is reprinted in John Nichols, *Biographical and Literary Anecdotes of William Bowyer, 1782* (New York & London, 1974), pp. 534-35.

15. Hanson, pp. 47 and 50.

16. Harris, "The Structure, Ownership and Control of the Press . . . ," in Boyce, Curran and Wingate (op. cit.) pp. 84-97, contains a good overview of government activities.

17. Blagden, p. 162.

18. For widows in the trade see Henry R. Plomer, *A Dictionary of the Printers and Booksellers who were at Work in Scotland and Ireland from 1668-1725* (Oxford, 1922), pp. 6, 15, 26, 107 and elsewhere. See also Blagden, pp. 95, 97, 162, 222.

19. *Stationers' Company Apprentices, 1641-1700*, D. F. McKenzie, ed. (Oxford, 1974). For Joanna Nye, see p. 114. I have gone strictly by first names in surveying numbers of female apprentices and the final dispositions of their apprenticeships.

20. *Stationers' Company Apprentices, 1701-1800*, D. F. McKenzie, ed. (Oxford, 1978). See for example pp. 111, 289, 306, 323.

21. Blagden, p. 162.

22. See *Stationers' Company Apprentices, 1641-1700*, p. 156, where Tace Sowle is noted as being "freed by patrimony." For information on her father see Leona Rostenberg, "Subversion & Repression: Robert Stephens, Messenger of the Press", in *Literary, Political, Scientific, Religious & Legal Publishing, Printing & Bookselling in England, 1551-1700: Twelve Studies* (New York, 1965), p. 356. John Dunton discusses her in his *Life and Errors of John Dunton* (New York, 1969), pp. 222-23. Among the works of Jane Lead published by Sowle are: *The Laws of Paradise Given Forth by Wisdom to a Transslated Spirit* (London, 1695) and *The Wonders of God's Creation Manifested, In the Variety of Eight Worlds; as they were made known Experimentally to the Author* (London, n.d.). I owe the information about Jane Lead's connection with Tace Sowle to Catherine Smith of Bucknell University.

23. Blagden, p. 162.

24. Ibid., p. 164.

25. Hodgson and Blagden, p. 80.

26. *London Evening Post* No. 2,540, Saturday 18 February 1744; quoted in Harris, "The London Newspaper Press . . .", p. 26.

27. For additional information on hawkers see ibid., Chapter 2; also Blagden, pp. 22, 147, 164-5, 169-70.

28. *Common's Journals*, V, 436, reads "that thirty thousand of these petitions were to come forth in print this day, and delivered to the Mercuries that cry about books." See also Fuller's *History of Cambridge*, "Circumforean Pedlars (ancestors to our modern Mercuries and Hawkers) which secretly vend prohibited pamphlets." These references from the *Compact Edition of the Oxford English Dictionary* (1971).

29. Harris, "The London Newspaper Press . . . ," pp. 42-3.

30. Dunton, p. 236.

31. Public Record Office, London, State Papers Domestic (hereafter SPD) 36/8 ff. 169-70.

32. Sutherland, p. 110.

33. Rostenberg, "English 'Rights and Liberties': Richard and Anne Baldwin, Whig Patriot Publishers," in her (op. cit.) Literary, Political, Scientific . . . Publishing . . . etc., p. 393.

34. Ibid., p. 408.

35. Ibid., pp. 411-12. Mrs. Manley appears on the masthead of the paper under the pseudonym "Mrs. Crackenthorpe."

36. Ibid., p. 370.

37. Estimate based on various sources including Tercentenary Handlist of English & Welsh Newspapers, Magazines and Reviews, facsimile reprint (London, 1966); R. S. Crane and F. B. Kaye, A Census of British Newspapers and Periodicals 1620-1800 (Chapel Hill, 1972); Powell Stewart, A Descriptive Catalogue of a Collection at the University of Texas; British Newspapers and Periodicals 1632-1800 (Austin, 1950). It must remain an estimate until adequate descriptive indexes are developed for all known eighteenth century newspapers and notably for the Burney Collection.

38. Tercentenary Handlist of English and Welsh Newspapers . . . , p. 35.

39. Ann Dodd was printer, publisher or sole distributor for the following papers: The Hermit (1711-1712), The Weekly Packet (1713-1721), The Old Whig (1710-1720), The Saint James Journal (1722-1723), The White Hall Evening Post (1721) and the Covent Garden Journal (1752), see Stewart, pp. 31, 112, 136, 162, 164.

40. The fullest description of congers and conger activity can be found in Norma Hodgson and Cyprian Blagden, The Notebook of Thomas Bennet and Henry Clements (1686-1719) with Some Aspects of Book Trade Practice, Oxford Bibliographical Society Publications, New Series, Vol. VI, 1953, pp. 67-100.

41. Ibid., p. 100.

42. Annotations on the Holy Bible. By a Select Body of Divines of the Church of England (London, 1735).

43. In this regard see the London Evening Post in the late 1730's, and the Daily Post for 1728-29. A consistently large volume of advertising by one bookseller in a particular journal probably indicates that that person has a share in ownership. In general ownership of newspapers was kept secret because of fear of prosecution. For more on this subject see Michael Harris, "London Printers and Newspaper Production During the First Half of the Eighteenth Century," Journal of the Printing Historical Society, Number 12, 1977-78, pp. 39-40.

44. More work is needed on the financial structure of early eighteenth century publishing and the precise relationship between newspaper advertising, a comparatively new phenomenon, and bookselling. At least one other possible explanation for the mercuries' frequent use of newspaper advertising is that they had fewer alternative business contacts than male booksellers, and used the newspaper columns to offset this disadvantage.

45. See, for example, Rostenberg, pp. 356, 393.

46. SPD 36/22, f. 12.

47. Sutherland, p. 117.

48. Quoted in Sutherland, p. 117.

49. Gillett, p. 588.

50. Ibid., p. 589.

51. Ibid., p. 589.

52. Ibid., p. 590.

53. SPD 36/8, f. 169.

54. SPD 36/8, f. 152.

55. SPD 36/8, f. 157.

56. SPD 36/8, f. 161.
57. SPD 36/8, f. 165.
58. SPD 36/8, f. 244.
59. Gillett, p. 621.
60. SPD 36/8, f. 169.
61. See the list of contributors in Nichols, pp. 496-97.
62. B. M. Add. MSS 33,054, ff. 189-90, quoted in Harris, "The London Newspaper Press" p. 45.
63. Harris, "London Printers and Newspaper Production," p. 38.
64. See SPD 36/8, f. 165.
65. C. H. Timperley, *A Dictionary of Printers and Printing* (London, 1839), p. 612 n.
66. Edward Deacon, *The Descent of the Family of Deacon of Elstowe and London* [etc.] (Bridgeport, Conn.: Privately printed, 1898), p. 339.
67. Nichols, pp. 534-5, contains a copy of Negus' List.
68. The sources differ on whether Elizabeth Nutt the mercury was Richard Nutt's mother or his wife. Deacon (p. 339) claims that Elizabeth Nutt was the daughter of Cassandra and Hugh Meeres. However, Harris, "The London Newspaper Press," p. 43, describes her as "the widow of printer John Nutt." There may have been two Elizabeth Nutts. See also Michael Treadwell, "London Printers and Printing Houses in 1705," *Publishing History*, Vol. VII, 1980, p. 30.
69. King's Bench Records, 28/131, ff. 22, 31.
70. SPD George II, 63, f. 216.
71. Henry R. Plomer (et al.), *A Dictionary of Printers and Booksellers who were at work in England, Scotland and Ireland from 1726-1775* . . . etc. (Oxford, 1932), entry on Sarah Nutt.
72. Hanson, p. 72.
73. Deacon, pp. 338-40, and Hanson, p. 72.
74. *DNB*.
75. The *DNB* argues against William Mears' being related to the other bookselling Mears, and *Stationers' Company Apprentices 1641-1700*, p. 74, would seem to bear this out.
76. Ralph Straus, *The Unspeakable Curll, Being Some Account of Edmund Curll, Bookseller, To Which is Added a Full List of his Books* (London, 1927), p. 294.
77. See Franco Venturi, *Italy and the Enlightenment: Studies in a Cosmopolitan Century* (London, 1972), pp. 63-102, for Radicati's life and association with English Commonwealth thinkers.
78. Deacon, pp. 344-5.
79. See SPD 36/8, ff. 152-170; also SPD 8/165, f. 154.
80. Straus, p. 296.
81. *Enthusiasm Display'd: Being a True Copy of a Most Learned, Conscientious and Devout Exercise, or Sermon* . . . *[Preached in 1649] by Lieutenant General Oliver Cromwell* (London, 1743).
82. Stewart, p. 112, supplies a description of the various editions of the *Old Whig*.
83. See for example, *The Adventures of Priests and Nuns; with some Account of Confessions and the Lewd Use They Make of Them* . . . etc. (published for . . . A. Dodd without Temple Bar, 1728).
84. See [John Henley], *Oratory Transactions No. 1* . . . *Occasion of the Oratory, Proving it an Episcopally and Legally Authorized Chapel of Ease and Correction to all Modern Churches* . . . etc. (Sold by E. Nutt, A. Dodd, N. Blanford, etc., 1728).
85. *DNB*
86. SPD 36/23, f. 134.
87. Straus, p. 295.
88. Ibid., pp. 300-301.
89. Saint-Hyacinthe's career and international connections are explored in Margaret C.

Jacob, *The Radical Enlightenment: Pantheists, Freemasons and Republicans* (London and Boston, 1981), pp. 187-93.

90. *Freedom of the Press: Six Tracts, 1712-1730* (New York and London, 1974).

91. See SPD 36/63, ff. 29, 36-7 for their interrogations by the Secretary of State's office.

92. A modern facsimile edition of this collection can be found in *The Rights of Authors: Two Tracts 1732-1738 and Freedom of the Press: Four Tracts 1740-1764* (New York and London, 1975).

93. Ibid., Sixth Tract, p. 10 (tracts individually paginated).

94. Ibid., p. 27.

95. Ibid., p. 33.

96. Ibid., p. 8.

97. Ibid., p. 21.

98. Ibid., p. 6.

99. Ibid., p. 33.

100. Ibid., pp. 24-5.

101. Ibid., p. 18.

102. Ibid., p. 8. The journal from which these pieces were excerpted had been proceeded against several times in the 1740s. Perhaps the "moderate" tone of this work is a deliberate effort to sidestep prosecution, though I think it more likely a propaganda device, an appeal to reason in the aftermath of the "Forty-five."

103. Mary Wollstonecraft, *A Vindication of the Rights of Women: With Strictures on Political and Moral Subjects* (London; 1792) pp. 26-31, 42-4.

104. Blagden, p. 231.

105. Ibid., pp. 251-52.

106. *Hodson's Booksellers, Publishers and Stationers Directory of 1855* (Oxford, 1972) lists a few women with newspaper stalls, apparently retailers, and only two women publishers out of more than 500 names. Neither of these women, a Mrs. Fairburn and a Miss Gibbs, appears to advertise, in stark contrast with the mercury women of the eighteenth century.

107. This change is exremely striking and can be readily seen in advertisements. One cited in Dunton, p. 216, ends with "to be sold by the hawkers of London." R. M. Wiles, *Serial Publication in England Before 1750* (Cambridge, 1957) reproduces a number of similar ads, e.g., from 1738, "subscribers to give notice to . . . any of the hawkers, or other persons, who serve out Books or Newspapers" (p. 315); 1737, "the persons who carry the news" (p. 311) and numerous other nongender-specific usages (pp. 296, 298, 349, and elsewhere). By contrast an unpaged advertisement in Hodsons refers to "Booksellers or newsmen in town or country."

108. Howe and Waite, pp. 169, 227.

Freemasonry, Women, and the Paradox of the Enlightenment

Margaret C. Jacob

In the Masonic lodges of the eighteenth century literate men invented a social setting wherein they could openly express their most enlightened ideals; inevitably, they also expressed the limitations and contradictions that plagued the practice of Enlightenment. Yet whatever their intellectual commitments or national setting, all official European lodges gave their assent to the British *Constitutions* of 1723 published by the Grand Lodge of London. That document proclaimed the ideals espoused by a rapidly growing membership: Baconian experimentalism coupled with adulation of the new science; religious toleration for all who worshipped the Grand Architect; court-centered but constitutional government; and equality within the lodge for "all brothers who meet upon the level." The *Constitutions* also rigorously excluded from membership on any level "women and bondsmen." The egalitarian ideal did not encompass women, nor did it include the servant class or, in practice, illiterate males or men who could not pay the entrance fees.[1]

English Masonic records from the early decades of the century indicate that lodge meetings were festive events where, even without women, wine and song prevailed and where the largely non-scientific brethren received occasional instruction in mathematics and simple mechanics in the presence of Newtonian scientists no less distinguished than Brook Taylor, Martin Folkes and Jean Desaguliers. This enthusiasm for the new science, so characteristic of Enlightenment culture, is reflected in the fact that over one-fourth of the early British Masonic membership also belonged to the

Margaret Jacob teaches at the City University of New York and is a fellow of The Institute for Research in History.

The author wishes to thank Phyllis Mack, Ruth Perry, Margaret Hunt, Gordon Silber, and Kathryn Sklar for their careful reading of this essay and their judicious comments.

Royal Society, and that the Society's official experimenter, De-saguliers, played a particularly active role in the lodges.[2] Freema-sonry's commitment to science extended well beyond the privacy of the lodge meetings. Perhaps paradoxically, this secret fraternity also willingly embraced the ideal of the public advancement of learning, and there remains throughout the history of eighteenth century Freemasonry a documentable link between encyclopedism and membership in the fraternity. The author of the first encyclo-pedia of the eighteenth century, Ephraim Chambers, was almost certainly a member of a London lodge; the French Huguenot edi-tors and publishers in The Hague who put out the 1720 edition of Bayle's *Dictionnaire* have now been shown to have had Masonic affiliations, and the abbé Claude Yvon, who has been described as the metaphysician of Diderot's great *Encyclopédie*, was a Freema-son in Amsterdam after his flight there in 1752.[3]

The essence of the Masonic mentality throughout the eighteenth century, I would suggest, lay precisely in its ability to espouse en-lightened and universal ideals that were in the context of most Eu-ropean societies as that time seen to be reforming, if not revolu-tionary, and then to live with, and indeed willingly embrace, a reality that contradicted those ideals. For example, the secret ritu-als and ceremonies of the lodges expressed a new ideal of social egalitarianism, yet on the question of women's equality and educa-bility most Masonic literature is generally ambivalent if not at mo-ments misogynist.[4] Masonic egalitarianism also faltered, it would seem, in the day-to-day practices of most lodges, where aristocrats and gentlemen were almost invariably accorded positions of lead-ership, in particular the title of Grand Master, while their social in-feriors tended to remain ordinary brothers. Of course secrecy itself could be seen, and was frequently attacked by anti-Masonic writ-ers, as the antithesis of tolerance and open constitutional govern-ment. But it is the contradiction presented by the sexual exclusiv-ity of Freemasonry which forms the subject of this essay, a subject suggested by my discovery of the earliest known record of a Ma-sonic lodge that attempted to apply its idealism to create a new, yet secret, reality and admitted women on an absolutely equal basis. The lodge that sought to create this new reality met in 1751 in The Hague, and well over fifty folio pages of its manuscript records have been preserved in the library of the Grand Lodge of The Netherlands housed in that city.[5] The lodge was established with the blessing of the official Grand Lodge, and the Grand Master of the Netherlands in 1751, Juste Gerard, Baron van Wassenaer, signed its *Livre de Constitution*. Possibly in recognition of this uniquely enlightened break with tradition, the new lodge took van Wassenaer's Christian name as its own, hence "la Loge de Juste". Official Freemasonry in The Netherlands began in 1734, although lodges did exist there considerably prior to that date. From the mid-1730's the official Dutch lodges subscribed to the 1723 British *Constitutions* complete with the exclusionary clause against women and bondsmen. Yet Dutch Freemasonry, like much of Continental Freemasonry during the second half of the eighteenth century, developed to a considerable degree independently of the London Grand Lodge. Predictably, the Dutch lodges identified themselves with a variety of political and cultural movements unique to their culture, yet not unrelated ideologically to their close English affiliations: Orangism, for example, particularly as fostered by the aristocratic leadership of certain lodges, more precisely by the Whig politicians William and Charles Bentinck, but also radical freethinking and republicanism, as exemplified by the pantheist, Jean Rousset de Missy (d. 1762), who was a prominent Amsterdam intellectual, a leading Master, and in his youth an associate of the English Commonwealth men, Toland and Collins. And it would seem that the newly-discovered lodge in The Hague also provided an outlet for a new sexual egalitarianism that had developed within a circle of that city's prominent aristocrats and theatre people.

Comprising no more than 35,000 souls in the mid-eighteenth century, The Hague was one of the most cosmopolitan cities in Western Europe. This ambiance was created by its diplomatic corps, its vast publishing industry, its governmental institutions, and its theatre-in-residence, the *Comédie Française*, which enjoyed a well-earned international reputation. For reasons we shall here attempt to establish its actresses and actors joined with William Bentinck and various other *haagse* gentlemen and one gentlewoman to form the first "mixed lodge" or "lodge of adoption"—as lodges that admitted men and women as equal members came to be known—to be found, as far as the records reveal anywhere in Europe.[6]

The manuscript records of this lodge reveal its constitution and membership list, and provide a set of initiation rituals, one of which is published here as an appendix. "La loge de Juste"—these records are entirely in French, the spoken language of polite soci-

ety in mid-eighteenth century Holland—invented its own rituals
by which the female and male members might express their equality, "fraternity", and mutual search for virtue and wisdom. Each
initiation ceremony brought the initiate closer to this virtue, which
in the ritual published here is equated with productivity and
the discipline of industry. The lodge had a variety of officers—
each title is listed in both the masculine and feminine—and all
ranks were available to both men and women. The language of
the rituals, almost without exception, is highly mystical and symbolic—squares, temples, symbolic fires and secret words abound
in the original texts—and that characteristic, making its appear-
ance quite early in the century relative to other Masonic records,
requires explication.[7] In this instance mystical language provides
one route for the expression of social behaviour which in the "real
world" of any European society at this time would have been
highly subversive.

From its very origins Freemasonry had attracted reformers. Predictably, by the 1740's there were Freemasons, usually writing
anonymously and in French, who demanded that women be admitted into the lodges on the grounds that sexual exclusivity contradicted the Masonic ideal of equality.[8] Quite apart from this idealism some pressure may also have been exerted from as early as the
1720's in England by anti-Masonic and homophobic writers who
attacked the male exclusivity of the lodges from that prejudiced
perspective. In the 1730's in The Netherlands homophobia reached
hysterical proportions, with over 200 men executed or imprisoned
on charges of sodomy. The Dutch Freemasons were occasionally
harassed by crowds caught up in that hysteria.[9] Yet none of these
pressures, not even the peculiarly violent ones exerted for a brief
time in The Netherlands, forced any other lodge there or elsewhere
in Europe to open its doors to female membership. In the 1740's
the French lodges specifically refused to admit women, and that
prohibition was not lifted officially until 1774. It would seem then
that external pressures do not adequately account for "la loge de
Juste". An explanation for its existence must be sought from the
limited records preserved by the Masons themselves, and from an
examination of the cultural milieu prevailing in The Hague at mid-
century which may have particularly affected the society of the
Bentincks and their friends.

The *mentalité* that permitted this lodge to exist in 1751, well before any other of its kind, commands our attention not only because it permitted a degree of sexual egalitarianism, however se-

cretive and fanciful its expression, but also because lodges like this one became fairly common in French aristocratic society by the 1770's and 80's. Those lodges are outside the scope of this essay, but their creation may indeed owe something to this original lodge established by men and women who travelled with their theatrical company throughout French-speaking Europe. There is a vast French literature from later in the century that testifies to the heated debate provoked by these experiments in sexual egalitarianism, a debate that shook the Masonic movement in those reforming and revolutionary decades. Why then did the genteel and educated, both aristocratic and bourgeois, choose to enact the fantasy of sexual equality?[10] What did "la loge de Juste" mean to its sisters and brothers?

Any explanation of the cultural milieu that helped to create this lodge requires that we delve briefly into the origins of Dutch Freemasonry and its role in the political life of the Dutch Republic. Freemasonry began officially in The Netherlands in 1734 when Vincent La Chapelle, *chef du cuisine* to William Charles Friso (1711-51), stadholder of Friesland and cousin of the long-deceased William III, King of England, established a lodge in The Hague. A few years prior to that establishment another lodge had met there under the sponsorship of the British Ambassador. As already indicated, Dutch Freemasonry at its origins possessed heavily Orangist associations, and the new lodges were closely linked to support for British interests on the Continent and for the Northern alliance against France. The States of Holland perceived that linkage almost immediately. Ever hostile to any revival of Orangism or to any possible interference with Dutch commercial interests in France, the States interrogated the Masonic leaders, closed down their lodge in 1735, and declared the movement illegal. That prohibition did not impede its rapid growth, nor could it stop Whig grandees like the Bentincks, one of whom, William Bentinck (1704-74), later became a sponsor of our lodge of adoption, from recruiting their friends and followers into the lodges. Neither could the anti-Orangist oligarchs of the States undermine the longstanding contacts that existed in the Republic between the opponents of French absolutism, many of them Huguenot refugees, and the English agents of various Whig governments. As early as the War of Spanish Succession (1701-13) Whig agents had been at work in the Low Countries, both north and south, establishing a network of spies, propagandists, journalists, and postal officials who did service first to the war effort and later to Walpole's government.[11]

Not only did these agents foster loyalty to Britain's role as the protector of Protestant Europe; they also exported the republicanism, anticlericalism and irreligion that had percolated on the fringes of the Whig party ever since the Restoration. The post-1689 Whig grandees had desperately wanted to ignore or forget that radical tradition, but their agents, men like John Toland and Anthony Collins, for example, could not always be controlled. Their subversive package of country-vs.-court radicalism and heterodoxy was tied, by Toland at least, to the project of starting a new civil religion. What better social setting for this worship of the secular than the old Masonic lodges which Toland had come to know, not through the artisans who had once met in that originally medieval guild, but through Whig gentlemen who now clubbed in the London lodges that met in taverns and alehouses. Artisan ceremonies reworked by merchants, politicians, party intellectuals and other sociable gentlemen could be molded to fit a variety of heterodox needs, not least of which could be a growing alienation from the world of social privilege and political power based solely upon birth.[12]

When Freemasonry was exported to The Netherlands by these Whig republicans, at least two decades before the British Ambassador established his lodge in The Hague, it had been given a radical and reforming slant that it would never entirely lose. The point is illustrated most succinctly by the career of the French Huguenot refugee, Jean Rousset de Missy (1686-1762), who became the leader of Amsterdam Freemasonry from the late 1730's until his exile in 1749 for revolutionary activities during the Dutch Revolution. From his earliest clandestine writings until well after his exile Rousset de Missy described himself as a "pantheist," having gotten that word from John Toland whom he had known in The Hague.[13] Rousset was also a republican with strongly democratic tendencies who did not shrink from popular insurrection. Despite being an agent for the Bentincks, in 1748 Rousset was at the head of an artisan movement in Amsterdam that demanded, but did not get, democratic reforms. The artisans sought to dismantle the iron grip of the ruling oligarchy and to open up offices to men of merit not of privilege. That was further than the Bentincks or the new stadholder, William IV, were prepared to go, and Rousset de Missy found himself exiled by his former paymasters, the Orangist leaders who had posed as reformers and who were also, incidentally, his Masonic, but rather more conservative, brothers.[14]

What this brief early history of Freemasonry up to the Dutch

Revolution of 1747 tells us for the history of the mixed male and female lodge we are describing is this: republicanism with strongly democratic tendencies, coupled with a variety of intellectual heresies, could be found prominently displayed in a few of the Dutch lodges. Yet the leaders of Dutch Freemasonry, who willingly sponsored our new lodge, were only interested in enlightened reform provided it served their interests and did not undermine the privileges of the traditional oligarchy. The Bentincks and their friends were among the small group of European aristocrats who read and admired the philosophes; both Charles and William Bentinck welcomed Rousseau and Diderot into their homes and they were also keenly interested in the new science.[15] Their Masonic affiliations allowed them social contact with groups normally excluded from elite society: merchants, minor government officials, publishers, Amsterdam Jews—all those men turn up in the membership archives.[16] Why not also women? Given this early history, is it surprising that Dutch Freemasons invented rituals and ceremonies to conjure up yet another secret heresy, the equality of the sexes? They in turn played this heresy out with the educated and theatrically gifted women who made up the *Comédie Française* in The Hague and with one or two ladies of good breeding there who also were tantalized by the fantasy.

The new lodge of adoption fits very well into the temper of the post-revolutionary Dutch Republic and also into what the Enlightenment must have been like when lived out by idealistic elites. This lodge of adoption certainly represented one expression of the enlightened search for equality among men and now women of reason and learning, and it self-consciously challenged traditional assumptions of masculine authority. But if we look closely at its membership and survey the grandeur of its proceedings, we will find that while "la loge de Juste" symbolically broadened the sexual distribution of power it remained well within the confines of elite society. In the privacy of its secret meetings this first lodge of adoption redefined the sexual and social mores of an aristocratic and bourgeois elite, but it never defied class boundaries nor publicly agitated for enlightened reforms. Within the microcosm of this lodge we are able to observe the strength and failings of the Enlightenment as a social phenomenon.

The Grand Master of The Netherlands, the Orangist Juste Gerard, Baron van Wassenaer (1716-53), who sponsored our lodge had been a loyal supporter of the revolution which restored the stadholderate. Probably as a result he had been made Grand Master of The Netherlands in 1748. Henri du Sauzet, an Amsterdam publisher and associate of Rousset de Missy, was chosen as his deputy grand master. But the new lodge of adoption was also headed by a Grand Mistress, an aristocratic woman of The Hague, Marianne, the Baroness d'Honstein (d. 1762), wife of Johannes, Baron van Honstein, a lieutenant captain in the Grand Regiment of the Republic. Her broad signature rests directly across from van Wassenaer's in the *Livre de Constitution* that established the lodge. The Grand Mistress appears also to have been a Catholic; baptismal records in The Hague show that the family was baptized and held their childrens' weddings in the Catholic Church. The family also had extensive property holdings in that city and made frequent recourse to notarized legal documents that survive in the municipal archives.[17] Could membership in "la loge de Juste" have been one means of affirming support for the stadholderate while also bridging the traditional gap that separated the Catholic aristocracy in The Netherlands from their Protestant and generally more influential counterparts?

The Baroness d'Honstein was, however, the only aristocratic woman among the female membership of the lodge which was largely composed of actresses in the prestigious troupe of the *Comédie Française*, with permanent headquarters in the city.[18] These women, about whom precious little historical information exists, arouse our greatest curiosity. What did this experience mean to them; why did they seek or accept Masonic membership? Since the property, birth, death and marriage records at the Gemeente Archief in The Hague reveal very little about them, we must assume that most were foreign born, or born in other Dutch cities, and that they lived and worked largely among themselves; they had already, perforce, established a fairly close-knit little community. We do know that some of the "sisters" who belonged to "la loge de Juste", were married to their fraternal "brothers"; at least this is true for Mmes. Van der Kaa, Derosimond and De Vos, while one sister, Marie Armand de Verteuil, was separated from her husband, and Mlle. Prevost was single at the time of her initiation.[19] Her mother was also a lodge member. Of the nineteen "sisters" who made up the lodge, a few, such as Elizabeth Forest and Mlles. Julien, Emilie and Le Blanc, all with the *Comédie*, made their permanent residence in Paris, while two came from Nantes.

Rosa Frazy (who signed her name Rosa Frasi) may have been Italian but she made her permanent residence in London.

Among the thirty-one "brothers" in "la loge de Juste", apart from the actors, were a significant number of local aristocrats: the Baron van Wassenaer, of course, and possibly one of his nephews; Ivan, Count de Golowkin; Willem Bentinck; Abraham, Baron de Suasso; and the 'Baron van Schield', along with the Prince van Baden. All were probably native aristocrats, the latter described as residing "dans ses états, et à la Haye". In addition five gentlemen were listed with their military titles, as lieutenants or captains of the Guard. They had joined with this company of French-speaking actors and actresses who catered to the most refined dramatic tastes of their age, doing serious drama, some by the French philosophes, along with *comédies* and Italian operas. Both players and patrons, among whom we must count the aristocratic and military *"frères"*, were fluent in the international language and culture of the eighteenth century.

Among the signatories of the initial *Livre de constitution* were the husband and wife team of Jean and Françoise Gravillon Baptiste Anselme. In the 1750's Jean was director of the *Comédie Française*; in the 1760s his wife and daughter assumed that role. Mlle. Rosette Baptiste, the daughter, also exercised her independence in a more libertine fashion, and she was widely regarded as the mistress of Jacques-Jean, Comte de Wassenaer d' Opdam (1724-79), one of the *frères* who in turn took a serious interest in the wellbeing of the *Comédie*.[20] The Anselme family appears also to have been Catholic, at least to the extent of baptising one of their children in the hidden Catholic Church that flourished discreetly on Oude Molstraat. The libertine reputation of Mlle. Anselme did not inhibit her fellow actors and actresses from joining with her in this lodge. The company had always suffered from accusations of libertinism and immorality; it is just possible that its definitions of respectability differed self-consciously from those that prevailed in the large society. Certainly the troupe was castigated for immorality, coupled with haughtiness, by clergy and scandal mongers alike; but with the assistance of powerful patrons in The Hague, not least in the late seventeenth century from the Stadholder, William III, the company generally flourished.[21]

In such a small city this extraordinary and new form of socializing, with its English associations, could not have gone unnoticed, especially when it entailed so many prominent citizens. The quasi-mystical ritual of "la loge de Juste" was probably suggested to the Grand Lodge by one William Mitchell (1727-92), a British officer of the Excise and possibly also a teacher of English who lived in The Hague and was a Masonic reformer. Mitchell had become taken with the new "Scottish" or philosophical, or mystical, free-masonry which criticized the Grand Lodge of London for its social exclusivity and which introduced new grades or philosophical de-grees of achievement, the grade of grand architect for example, into Masonic proceedings.[22] The records of "la loge de Juste" in-clude Mitchell's name and make specific reference to "une maçon-nerie nouvelle, sous le titre de maçonnerie écossoise, divisée en deux grades, sous les nomes d'architecte et de grand architecte." Within the year this innovation in the social life of Hague society apparently did come to the attention of a French abbé who pro-ceeded to write a satire against it.

Without mentioning Freemasonry, abbé Coyer's attack, pub-lished in 1751 and then in 1752 in The Hague, makes specific ref-erence to one Captain Mitchell and "ses frères", to the English ori-gin of their "frivolity", to their interest in mathematics, and then quite pointedly to what he calls the courtesans in their midst.[23] The burden of the attack centers on the forms of socializing adopted by this coterie, on their imitation of aristocratic manners while at the same time valuing merit, not birth, among them-selves.[24] Indeed, the abbé argues, they have taken elegance of manners to the point of a religion and in their temple, while des-pising all other religions, they worship the sun and the moon. They have prohibited polygamy, but in fact they practice it, and in the process have made it possible for "the inferior sex" to lose their virtue with decency.[25] It is hard to be sure that the angry abbé had "la loge de Juste" firmly in mind when he penned his treatise, but it seems a possibility. And predictably, of the many innovative customs practiced by this lodge, or by some other simi-larly egalitarian group, the mixing of the sexes on an equal foot-ing, even more than the apparent irreligion, gave him the greatest offence.

But the actors and actresses of the Comédie had managed to give offence in other quarters besides the clergy, and to do so pre-cisely because of their social behaviour. One of their number, or one of their supporters, publicly attacked the social prejudice that prevailed against actors and actresses, even claiming that snobbery was worse in The Hague than in Paris. Actors and actresses, he or she proclaimed, were as good as anybody else "for anyone can have titles and riches but talents are a gift from heaven and such gifts are always respectable."[26] That defense was answered by another published tract that bitterly attacked the company, not for its acting, which was acknowledged to be sometimes quite good, but for its social arrogance. These actors and actresses, wrote the author, think that merit and not birth, should count in the eyes of society, and in so doing they threaten "the maintenance of law and public security". "Despite the republican spirit and independence that reigns here," this detractor of the *Comédie* argues, "one is still strongly persuaded that subordination is necessary. Each citizen is useful and respectable in his place (dans son état)."[27] Apparently this hostile critic did not know that these would-be social reformers were fraternizing in secret with some of the most elite elements in this cosmopolitan city. The plays by the philosophes performed by the troupe of the *Comédie* complemented its familiarity with a secret fraternity that possessed a distinctively egalitarian, even enlightened, ideology to which the leaders of the new Orangist government gave their allegiance. In that secret world the actors, and even more the actresses, could indeed practice the equality and respectability to which they aspired. The rituals of their lodge glorified the worker and "the work", and indeed they believed that real, not only symbolic, labor provided the evidence for their merit and talent.

One other possible link between the secret Masonic lives lived by these actors and actresses and the ideals proclaimed by the philosophes in their plays should also be mentioned. Throughout his life Diderot argued for the theatre as an agent of social change, as a podium for enlightened thinking as well as an occasion for emotional release.[28] It would rival the pulpit, indeed surpass its force, he said, by acting out ideals that contradicted those most commonly preached by the clergy. Such enthusiasm for the educative value of the theatre did not begin with eighteenth century reformers. Frances Yates found seventeenth century actors and actresses who advocated Rosicrucianism and used the stage as a podium to spread that mystical gospel.[29] Intellectual links exist between the reforming zeal of that seventeenth century movement and later eighteenth century Freemasons, who largely rediscovered the Rosicrucians and grafted them on to their mythical history. Who would know those reforming traditions in European theatrical history better than actors and actresses themselves, especially if they were keenly resentful, as our troupe in The Hague appears to have been, of society's bigotry and superstition? And perhaps this passion to act out alternatives to social convention extended beyond those evenings on the stage when one got the opportunity to perform the new, philosophical plays emanating from Paris; perhaps these actors and actresses also wanted to create for themselves an alternative fantasy of enlightenment that could at least have the illusion of reality. "Without distinction of birth", as the manuscript records of "la loge de Juste" proclaim, "the brothers and sisters" will deport themselves "without vice, in order to augment the good manners of society and to dissipate the shadows that cover the eyes of the profane." They declare that the members will attempt to spread themselves "over the surface of the earth".[30]

Without detracting from the zeal and originality displayed in these documents of "la loge de Juste", some historical antecedents for this sort of sexually egalitarian socializing should be acknowledged. These precedents are particularly relevant because the lodge itself had an interest in such antecedents and collected anecdotes and written "tableaux" about them. In the late seventeenth century The Hague had been a center for upper-class *préciosité*, with its feminist and gallican associations.[31] Also, within Dutch republican and bourgeois circles associated with John de Witt in the 1660's at least one club with important intellectual interests had admitted men and women as equal members. Reference to that club is made in the manuscripts of "la loge de Juste" where an unknown writer makes a brief attempt to patch together its history.[32] Also by the late 1730's, first in Austria and then in France, various orders of aristocratic women had sprung up that imitated aspects of Masonic proceedings. The *Ordre des Mopses* is one such example in which our lodge had an interest, but it should be sharply distinguished from "la loge de Juste" and its egalitarian socializing. In that order brothers paid court in mock-heroic fashion to stereotypical sisters with stereotypical names—the married woman (*Soeur Aimable*), the frigid beauty (*Soeur Brillante*), the lady of love and laughter (*Soeur Gracieuse*). The *mopses* are barely distinguishable from their faithful dogs, the *mops*, who were the mascots of the order, and in both cases fidelity seems to have been their only noteworthy achievement. The Masonic sisters and brothers appear to have been interested mainly in the order's initiation ceremony.[33]

Yet for all of these precedents and intellectual traditions, "la loge de Juste" must be acknowledged as unique in its time. Its records also portray some sense on the part of its organizers that this lodge required special ceremonies and protection. Recognized and financially subsidized by the Grand Lodge, the new lodge began its constitution "in the name of the Grand Architect of the universe . . . under the most exalted and wise protection of the Baron Wassenaer." But ultimate responsibility for the welfare of the lodge lay with the Baroness d'Honstein. In the manner of the Scottish rite, this lodge was to have three degrees for both women and men, "apprenti, apprentrice; compagnon, compagnone; maître et maîtresse".[34] Just as did Freemasons all over Europe, the ladies and gentlemen of The Hague were to assume symbolically the gloves and apron of the skilled artisan, while striving to augment their skills by the industrious cultivation of moral virtue and intellectual achievements. In addition, the lodge's officers were both women and men: a *député maitre* and *députée maitresse*, *un grand surveillant* and *une grande surveillante*, *un grand secrétaire* and *grande secrétaire*, *un grand orateur* and *grande oratrice*, *un grand trésorier* and *grande trésorière*.[35] The annual elections to those offices were to be without "distinction of birth", and what is most important the manuscript records indicate a complete sexual equality in all the lodge's rituals.

In keeping with the Scottish form of this lodge, "la Juste" also initiated its members into a special degree, the grade of architect, which appears at this time to have been unique to that lodge. As the initiation ceremony printed in the appendix reveals, both women and men officers participated in this special ritual. Indeed this was a degree to which only masters or mistresses could be admitted, and its recipient, who had to be initiated by a member of the Grand Lodge, vowed to practice virtue, silence, charity, fidelity and temperance. In this instance a language more gnostic than scientific provided a bridge that permitted these women and men to become something other than they were, to reach out through gestures and words for an illumination of the spirit that would be both individually and, more important, socially experienced. The initiation rite closed with "the kiss of reason", and the degree carried with it a secret password "Nejusrimatea" by which its holders might be identified. As the manuscript catechism that accompanies the degree ceremony explains, the word signified "production", and the Venerable One, representing the Grand Lodge, and the *surveillant* were meant to chant out the meaning of that universal Masonic work which begins and ends in the symbolic center of the lodge.[36]

At the center rests the temple of virtue, and in its center shines a primitive light, the light of reason. "La loge de Juste" took a small animal, the ermine with its precious coat and fastidious manner, as a symbol of its proud search for virtue and reason. Adorning a pictorial representation of the animal was to be the motto, "I would rather die than defile myself." In the ritual for reception of a master and mistress the virtue sought is specifically identified as Christian, but in all other places in the records virtues are simply named, with discrimination being made solely between the non-Mason, "le prophane masculin, et feminin" and those initiated into "la lumière de tout les grades de maçonnerie d'adoption."[37]

This cosmopolitan universalism, here defined to include women, was the hallmark of Masonic idealism and was very much in evidence in Dutch Freemasonry during the middle decades of the eighteenth century. As Rousset de Missy, that philosophical radical and leader among Amsterdam Freemasons, remarked in one of his private letters, "anyone can be a Freemason, except a Jesuit."[38] Likewise the manuscript records of "la loge de Juste" speak of "the lodges of the masonry of adoption" which "will establish themselves in the United Provinces."[39] Although there is no evidence that more than this one lodge was ever established, the possibility was contemplated and indeed encouraged in the official constitution. The 1751 Masonic *Almanac*, published for the use of all Dutch Freemasons, even printed toasts by which the brothers and sisters in such a lodge might begin their "Fête de Table". For example, a brother proclaims: "Drink to our amiable sisters, my brothers", and he is answered by a sister, "drink, to our tender brothers". Very shortly all are joined in a song that proclaims "our perfect union."[40] In that same *Almanac* a Mlle. de Brouquère is listed as a "grand maitresse", and since her name does not appear in the records of "la loge de Juste" it is just possible that at least one other lodge of adoption had been established in The Netherlands.

In addition members of the Grand Lodge published in 1751 a special, and now very rare, songbook, *Chansons de l'Ordre de l'Adoption ou la Maçonnerie des Femmes*, dedicated to "the sisters of the fraternity spread over the surface of the earth." It consists of fifteen melodies and seventeen songs, all of the latter having been written by two *frères*, Corbin and Parmentier, both members of "la loge de Juste", and intended by them to be sung to well-known tunes for which the musical notation is provided.[41] Although the songs are interesting in themselves, what commands our fascination is a preliminary discourse affixed to them and written by Saint-Etienne, the deputy master of "la loge de Juste". He writes for his Masonic brothers, to convince them of the value of this new "lodge of adoption". The passions, in particular vanity, ambition and self-regard, he claims, have taken hold in the heart of man, and these are only moderated by "the sciences". The passions have produced "in various nations a profound ignorance," and that blindness has prevented thousands of men from seeing that women "have been formed to be [men's] faithful companions, sharing in the happiness, the pleasure of their actions", and that they are "one of the most beautiful ornaments . . . in the order of nature's perfections."[42] Saint-Etienne likens this widespread ignorance to that found in Plato's cave, and as a result of its perpetuation for many centuries "masons would not admit their wives into their lodges."

But the ignorance of men, Saint-Etienne continues, must be dispelled not in far away places but "in their Republic." A small group of citizens on this earth have escaped this ignorance, and "they are distinguished and known under the name of masons, perfect friends, faithful compatriots and guardians of the temple of virtue and truth." These men alone "by their wise discretion, in the practice of their labors, have maintained the deference and affection which is due to the perfect companion of man [i.e. to woman]." Out of the extreme sexual exclusivity of all other lodges, Saint-Etienne manages a rhetorical exit simply by claiming that "the light" has finally dispelled the darkness; "our profound study in the art of masonry has enabled us to find a true method of perfecting our buildings [*nos édifices*]: it is by the assistance of our sisters." With them we shall build "the school of manners, the temple of virtue."

This brief discourse is a powerful example of the resourcefulness of eighteenth century Masonic rhetoric in justifying digressions from social convention or in articulating departures from conventional moral or religious wisdom. Once you are in the temple of virtue, compelled by the primitive light, hermetically sealed off from the ignorant and the profane, you can embrace brothers and even sisters with whom you have little in common save your shared idealism, and you can, as Saint-Etienne does, argue for the universal truth and applicability of your actions.

But this Masonic ideal of universalism bore little relation to the real barriers to membership that income or the absence of surplus wealth must have presented. Admission to "la loge de Juste" was a costly matter. Aside from the gold plated jewelry depicting the sun and the moon that grand masters and mistresses wore, silk and taffeta accessories were also a part of a member's basic attire.[43] The members may have embraced the symbols of the workman's uniform, but in rendering their aprons in taffeta and their gloves in silk the brothers and sisters also symbolically repudiated the sweat, dirt and hard work that is the lot of the worker. At the *Comédie Française* where so many of the brothers and sisters were employed, a stagehand with some technical skill who arranged the scenery between acts was paid a little over six guilders a day for four days of work in 1752.[44] But since the company performed irregularly that sum could not be expected on a daily basis. In the same year the best seat in the theatre was 3 fl. for one performance, although places were available for less than a guilder.[45] In 1750 a worker in the shipbuilders' guild in Amsterdam could hope to earn 1.4 fl. per day for work at the highest wage rate.[46] Unfortunately, the actual income of any one of the actors or actresses in the *Comédie* cannot be determined from available records because the company negotiated for space, etc. as a company and then divided up the profits fairly equally among themselves. But we do know that the actors and actresses of the prestigious company lived well and kept servants, and that at this time a good actor on the Amsterdam stage could earn up to 1000 fl. a year.[47]

Membership expenses in "la loge de Juste" were not affordable on the wages of a day laborer, but the lodge was open to the well-born, the highly remunerated professional classes and to properous merchants, all of whom could probably manage to find the money for a woman's taffeta apron at 5.5 fl., or a man's at 3 fl., and a trowel at 1 fl., to name only the most important items in the Masonic wardrobe.[48] But expenses only began there. The lodge required stationery, plates, and drinking cups, not to mention the services of cooks, waiters and laundresses. There was, of course, an initiation fee that could run from the 21 fl. paid by M. van den Bergh (which was less than half what a foreign worker paid to get into the Amsterdam shipbuilders' guild),[49] to the 78 fl. paid by M. et Mad. van Belle, who were incidentally prominent and respected Protestants, to the highest sum of 52 fl. paid by an individual, predictably by Count Bentinck. The three boy servants who waited on the lodge members at their meetings each received a guilder, or three guilders a month. In 1751 the cook who prepared the Easter lamb received 3 fl. Pairs of gloves were also given gratis to some members, but it is hard to know why. The total cost for opening this new lodge came to 592.2 fl., with its initial income equalling only 439.5 fl. The Grand Lodge paid the difference, and incidentally it is not clear that every brother and sister had to pay an initiation fee. In short, membership in "la loge de Juste" for the prosperous was costly but not exorbitant and, within limits, differing degrees of prosperity were accepted and contributions reduced accordingly.

Can we say anything else specifically about the women who invested in "la loge de Juste" and through its ceremonies proclaimed their symbolic equality as "*soeurs*" and "*maîtresses*"? The women of the *Comédie Française* were working women living an unusually cosmopolitan and highly mobile life-style. In some cases they were foreign born, and with their company they would also have travelled extensively in France and the Low Countries. In that sense they already lived as those citizens of the world proclaimed in the philosophic literature. All of them had to be shrewd business women and they possessed more than a passing familiarity with literature and the arts. But most especially they were students of manners and dress; they were already skilled at turning fantasy into reality.

The importance of the fact that so many members of "la loge de Juste" were theatrical people cannot be over-emphasized. It required no small imagination to create the equality of the sexes, and to express it in new Masonic rituals to be staged with serious and decorous formality by the participants. And does not the experience of the stage reveal especially to the players and hopefully to the audience the relativity and historicity of mores, sexual and otherwise? Furthermore, in these symbolic actions a camaraderie and economic interdependence that already existed among the troupe could be given expression, while sexual equality could be embraced by the players and their many friends, women and men who at least at the moment of their symbolic actions accepted it as both reality and ideal.

As social beings the women of "la loge de Juste" experienced the Enlightenment in secret. Yet theirs was still a more public expression than was possible for most women for whom "enlightenment" was largely confined to the printed word read in the privacy of their homes. It is little wonder that feminist writers throughout the century, from Mary Astell to Mary Wollstonecraft, responded to enlightened culture with decided ambivalence. But we do not sense any of their discomfort or reservation in the elaborate rituals, songs and catechisms chanted by *les soeurs* with *les frères*. There were moments in the eighteenth century, such as the one we have just described, when the Enlightenment endorsed a new social and economic reality that afforded greater freedom and equality to a very few women. But that endorsement on the level of social experience was most uncommon and perhaps only given in privacy, or even in secrecy, and then within very restricted class boundaries. The extension of fraternity and equality into the lives of the mass of the people was perceived by enlightened men, and possibly also by enlightened women, as a process fraught with great danger. Yet it must be acknowledged that among those eighteenth century reformers most likely to embrace that danger might be men and women like our brothers and sisters of "la loge de Juste" who found within Freemasonry a set of ideals and a context within which they could openly, yet still in secrecy, defy conventional prejudices and the prevailing social reality.

REFERENCES

1. M. Paillard, ed. *The English and French Masonic Constitutions*, (London, 1940), pp. 38, 56. For the attitude of present-day British Freemasons, who even condemn the American ladies auxiliary, The Order of the Eastern Star, see A.S. Frere, *Grand Lodge, 1717-1967*, (Oxford, printed for the Grand Lodge, 1967), p. 164. On illiteracy see Edward Oakley, *A Speech Deliver'd to the Worshipful Society of Free and Accepted Masons, at A Lodge, held at Carpenters' Arms in Silver Street, Golden Square, the 31st December, 1728*, found most easily in *Cole's Constitutions*, William J. Hughan, ed., (Leeds, 1897) p. 29, urging the lodge to take care not to admit the irreligious, the lewd, or "persons illiterate or of mean capacities." And see a tract that speaks for the Grand Lodge, Anon., *A Defense of Freemasonry, As practiced in the Regular Lodges both foreign and domestic, Under the Constitution of the English Grand Master* . . . London, 1765, p. 36, against the egalitarian Masonic reformers of the 1760's.

2. J. P. Clarke, "The Royal Society and Early Grand Lodge Freemasonry," *Ars Quatuor Coronatorum*, 80, 1967, pp. 110-19.

3. See my *The Radical Enlightenment: Pantheists, Freemasons and Republicans*, (London and Boston, 1981), chapter five, for Prosper Marchand, et al., and p. 259 for Yvon.

4. For misogyny see M. Paillard, ed., *The English and French Masonic Consitutions*, pp. 38, 56, "no woman, no eunuch;" for progressive views see *The Perjur'd Free Mason Detected* (London, 1723) and *The Generous Free-Mason* (London, 1731); for ambivalence see D. Knoop, G. P. Jones, D. Hamer, eds., *The Early Masonic Catechisms*, (Manchester, 1963), pp. 226-39. And in favor of women being made Freemasons, Thomas Davenport, *Love to God and Man inseparable . . . before . . . Free and Accepted Masons . . . 27 December 1764 . . .* Birmingham, printed for the author by J. Sketchley, 1765, p. 240, in G. Oliver, ed., *The Golden Remains of the Early Masonic Writers*, (London, 1847).

5. The Library of the Grand Lodge of The Netherlands, 22 Fluwelen Burgwal, The Hague, folder marked *Livre de Constitution* containing approximately sixty folio pages (some blank) and made available by the kindness of the librarian, B. C. van Uchelen. And see his very useful "De Vrijmetselarij en de Vrouw," *Thoth*, 26, 1975, pp. 145-58.

6. For The Hague as a town and its development see *Enige Grondslagen voor de Stedebouwkundige ontwikkeling vans s'Gravenhage*. Uitgave van het Gemeetebestuur van s'Gravenhage, 1948, p. 325, gives population development, ie, 1622, 17,430 souls; 1730, 33-34,000; 1755 to 1773, ± 41,500. On the Masonic membership of Willem IV see E. A. Boerenbeker, "The Relations between Dutch and English Freemasonry from 1734 to 1771" in *Ars Quatuor Coronatorum*, 83, 1970, pp. 149-192; on Amsterdam in 1748 and the Freemasons see Antonio Porta, *Joan en Gerrit Corver. De politieke macht van Amsterdam (1702-1748)*, (Assen, 1979), pp. 207-11, 232-265. On the earliest lodge established in The Netherlands see Hugo de Schampheleire, "Une Loge maçonnique à Rotterdam, fondée avant 1721-22", *Lias*, viii, 1981, pp. 79-85.

7. For mysticism and Masonic symbolism see Ronald D. Gray, *Goethe, The Alchemist*, (Cambridge, 1952); and for a wealth of such literature see the catalogue of the library of the Grand Lodge of The Netherlands, George Kloss, *Beschrijving der Verzamelingen van het Groot-Oosten der Nederlanden*, (The Hague, 1888). A portion of this library will soon appear on microfiche published by a firm called Interdocumentation, Leiden.

8. On the French phenomenon, see Elaine Brault, *La franc-maçonnerie et l' émancipation des femmes*, (Paris, 1953) [not very good]; G.H. Luquet, *La franc-maçonnerie et l' état au XVIIIme siècle*, (Paris, 1964), pp. 58-65, 205-07, 227; Louis Guillemain de Saint-Victor, *Recueil précieux de la Maçonnerie Adonhiramite*, (Philadelphie [Paris], 1787), pp. 132-41, gives songs used in lodges of adoption, and vol. III which bears the title, *La vraie maçonnerie d'adoption*. That volume also appears under the title *Amusemens d'une société innombrable dans laquell on compte des héros, des philosophes* published in 1779. This may be the same as *La Vraie maçonnerie d'adoption; précédée de quelques Réflexions sur les Loges irrégulières & sur la Société civile . . . dé diée aux dames*. Par un Chevalier de tous les Ordres Maçonniques. Philadelphie, chez Philarethe, 1783, which contains a philosophical justification for women's participation, as well as songs sung in the lodges of adoption. Perhaps the earliest tracts describing the French lodges of adoption are [Anon.], *L'Adoption ou la Maçonnerie des Femmes en Trois Grades, "A La Fidélite"*, n.p., chez le Silence, 1775. [Colophon: "Ce Livre se trouve à la Haye, chez P. Gosse & Pinet, & à Genève, chez I. Bardin."]; and *La Maçonnerie des Femmes*, Londres, 1774. Cf. Albert Lantoine, *Histoire de la franc-maçonnerie française*, (Paris, 1925), pp. 375-79; Eugen Lennhoff and Oskar Posner, *Internationales Freimaurerlexikon*, (Vienna, 1932), pp. 42, 17-18,289. In D. Knoop, G. P. Jones, D. Hamer, eds., *The Early Masonic Catechisms*, (Manchester, 1963) there is a reprint of a 1724 pamphlet, *A Letter from the Grand Mistress*, published by John Harding. It is almost cerainly spurious in relation to women's role but it raises some interesting questions which will be discussed in the course of this paper. An easily accessible discussion of the French lodges can be found in Daniel Ligou, ed.,

88   WOMEN AND THE ENLIGHTENMENT

Dictionnaire universel de la francmaçonnerie, (Paris, 1974), p. 15. See also G. Jogand-Pages [Leo Taxil], *Les Soeurs maçonnes*, (Paris, 1886), pp. 12-18. And for a defense of these Dutch lodges of adoption when under attack during the Napoleonic occupation, see *Tweede Memoire van Defensie van de A.'. □.'. L'Union Royale . . . werkende onder het G..'. O..'. van Holland.*

9. *The Free-Masons; an Hudibrastick Poem*, (London, 1723), p. 20; and on riots in The Hague against the Free-Masons linking them with suspected homosexuality see *Daily Advertiser*, December, 1735. See also *Europische Mercurius*, 1730, I, pp. 283-304, II, 289-304. On Masonic egalitarianism in general see J. M. Roberts, *"Liberté, égalité, fraternité*: sources and development of a slogan," *Tijdschrift voor de studie van de verlichting*, 4, 1976, pp. 329-370, and in the same volume, which is devoted to Freemasonry, see Hugo de Schampheleire, "L'Égalitarisme maçonnique et la hiérarchie sociale dans les pays-bas autrichiens," pp. 433-504. See also the use of the Masonic symbolism for *égalité* during the French Revolution, E. H. Gombrich, "The Dream of Reason: Symbolism in the French Revolution", *The British Journal for Eighteenth-Century Studies*, vol. 2, no. 3, 1979, p. 202.

10. On elite mentality in general see Harry Payne, "Elite versus Popular Mentality in the Eighteenth Century", in Roseann Runte, ed., *Studies in Eighteenth-Century Culture*, vol. 8, 1979, pp. 3-32, and his earlier *The Philosophes and The People* (New Haven, 1976). Cf. Maurice Aguilhon, *Pénitents et Francs-Maçons de l'ancienne Provence: Essai sur la sociabilite méridionale* (Paris, 1968).

11. *The Radical Enlightenment*, chapter five.

12. See Harry Carr, *Lodge Mother Kilwinning, No. O. A. Study of the Earliest Minute Books*, (London, published by the Quatuor Coronati Lodge, 1961), and for medieval masons see D. Knoop, *The Medieval Mason*, (Manchester, 1967).

13. *The Radical Enlightenment*, p. 215 and passim.

14. Nico J. J. de Voogd, *Die Doolistenbeweging te Amsterdam in 1748*, De Vroede, Utrecht, 1914, *passim*. In general for the Revolution see P. Geyl, "Holland and England during the War of the Austrian Succession", *History*, 10, 1925, pp. 47-51. And Rousset de Missy can now be identified as the editor of the 1755 Amsterdam edition of the French translation of Locke's *Two Treatises* complete with new notes. See *Du gouvernement civil, par Mr. Locke. Traduit de l'anglois. Cinquieme Edition . . . augmentée de quelques Notes. Par L.C.R.D.M.A.D.P.* (my italics for Rousset de Missy), (Amsterdam, 1755), an example on p. 10 n, "Cette restriction est encore nécesaire; et on doit y faire bien attention, en se souvenant que c'est ceque dictent les loix de la Nature, *dans l'État de Nature*". The most extensive treatment of Rousset occurs in J. Sgard, ed., *Dictionnaire des Journalistes*, (1976), listed alphabetically, and Dr. W. Kat, *Een Grootmeestersverkiezing in 1756 uit het archief van de A.L. "La Bien Aimée"*, Eigen uitgave van de Loge, The Hague, 1974, prints Rousset's letters to the lodge.

15. For the Bentincks, see *The Radical Enlightenment*, pp. 198-201, 235-38, 261. On another, darker side of Bentinck's relations with women see Joanne Boeijen, *et al.*, "Notre Misère est Générale. Gedachten van Charlotte-Sophie Bentinck over de positie van de vrouw", *Documentatieblad Werkgroep 18e Eeuw*, no. 44, 1979. The tragically unhappy portrait of their marriage given by Charlotte-Sophie Bentinck highlights the point about fantasy and reality.

16. The Grand Lodge of the Netherlands, "Annales de Dagran" and "Kronick Annales."

17. Gemeente Archief, The Hague, records of births and marriages, Nr. 1773 and 1774.

18. See J. Fransen, *Les comédiens français en Hollande au XVIIe et au XVIIIe siècles*, (Paris, 1925; reprint ed. Geneva, 1978), p. 327 n makes mention of an all-male lodge of actors in 1761 but not of this earlier lodge of adoption. Yet this book is invaluable as a guide to identifying these women. The records for the men's lodge, *L'Égalité de Frères*, are also in the Grand Lodge's library. The lodge appears to have begun in 1763, not 1761. The only short discussion of our lodge of adoption in print, other than the brief mention given in the

article cited in note 5, appears in Robert Strathern Lindsay, *The Royal Order of Scotland*, Edinburgh, published by the Grand Lodge of the Royal Order of Scotland, 1971, pp. 39, 61-65. See also James Fordyce, *The Temple of Virtue, A Dream*, London, 1759, a utopian fantasy obviously based on Scottish Freemasonry, where women are given significant roles within the temple of virtue (pp. 59-64) and their virtue is defined as both domestic and republican.

19. Ibid., pp. 330, 304, 309.

20. Ibid., p. 316.

21. Fransen, p. 210-11; 232-6, 251.

22. On Scottish freemasonry as simply a more elaborate form of Masonic philosophizing see J. M. Roberts, *The Mythology of the Secret Societies*, (London, 1972), pp. 94-100, and C.H. Chevalier, "Maçons écossais au XVIIIe siècle" in *Annales historiques de la révolution française*, v. 41, 1969, pp. 393-408. Cf. Paul Naudon, *Histoire et rituels des hauts grades maçonniques. Le Rite écossais ancien et accepte*, (Paris, 1966), pp. 61-62. By 1761 there were at least twenty-five grades within French Freemasonry of which the 19th grade was that of grand architect.

23. Mr. L'abbé Coyer, *Découverte de l'isle frivole*, La Haye, 1751, pp. 8, 11, 15, 19.

24. *Découverte*, p. 38: "Chez les Frivolités comme en Europe on parle beaucoup du mérite. Il faut des hazards singuliers pour en tirer parti: mais c'est un point bien décidé qu'il est plus avantageux d'être goûté." "Il n'en est pas de l'honneur comme du mérite." On Coyer see L. Adams, "Coyer and the Enlightenment", *Studies on Voltaire and the Eighteenth Century*, v. 123, 1974. It is possible that Coyer had also heard of *l'ordre de la Felicité*, a non-Masonic organization that began in France in 1742. But Mitchell had no known association with it. Coyer was in the United Provinces in 1747 during the War of Austrian Succession (Adams, p. 24) and the tone of his tract is chatty and familiar, always implying that he has "seen" or been told about, these "frivolities", and he knew the chevalier de Ramsay, perhaps the most prominent French Freemason, after Montesquieu, in the Enlightenment. There is an English translation of this tract, *A Discovery of the Island Frivola*, (London, 1750), but the date does not conform to any known French text and appears to be wrong by at least a year.

25. *Découverte*, p. 38: "A l'arrivée de l'Admiral (the leader of this group) on formoit un éstablissement où le sexe subalterne pourroit perdre sa vertu avec decénce." p. 41: "Ils adorent le Soleil; ils voudroient bien l'aimer, mais la façon les embarrasse. Lui doivent ils de l'amour à cause qu'il les échauffe et les éclaire, ou parce qu'il est chaud et lumineux en lui-même? C'est une dispute de cent ans. Ils ont proscrit la Poligamie, parce qu'il n'y a qu'un soleil et qu'une lune: mais un mari fait bien qu'il doit tâcher de plaire à plusieurs femmes, et les femmes auroient un air bien sauvage sie elles s'en fâchoient. Un dogme capital de leur Religion, c'est de condamner toutes les autres."

26. *Amusements de la Toilette ou Recueil des Faits . . . les plus singuliers tragiques et comiques de l'amour passés en Hollande en Angleterre et en France . . .* (The Hague, 1756), I, pp. 121-28, in particular, p. 127, where the reference to the "mason" is not, I suspect, accidental: "Ce sont des particuliers . . . se peut-il qu'il y ait des Hommes qui ayant l'orgueil de croire que la Nature les ait mis au dessus d'un Maçon ou d'un Boulanger. Un automate, un . . . Que dirai-je? Tous les Hommes peuvent avoir des titres et des richesses; mais les talens, sont des dons du Ciel, and les dons du Ciel sont toujours respectacles (sic)." These pages are dated 1755; note that the publisher also did many works by Rousset de Missy.

27. *L'Anti-Calomniateur, ou défense du theatre françois de la Haye*. Liège, 1755, p. 25.

28. Arthur M. Wilson, *Diderot*, Oxford, Oxford University Press, 1972, pp. 262-64, 330-31.

29. Frances A. Yates, *Shakespeare's Last Plays*, London, Routledge & Kegan, Paul, 1975, pp. 123-31. I owe this point to Phyllis Mack.

30. *Livre de Constitution*, ff. 10 r.&v.

31. J. A. Dijkshoorn, *L'influence française dans les moeurs et les salons des provinces-unies*, (Paris, 1925) (*proefschrift* for the University of Groningen), p. 213-19.

32. *Livre de Constitution*, The Grand Lodge of The Netherlands. This is a different hand from the one that wrote the *Livre*; the ms is entitled "Amelie grande Maitresse du pretieux Orde de l'Union de La joye" and it appears to be a copy of a 1653 letter by one of its leaders. Cf. Haijo Zwager, *Waarover Spraken Zij? Salons en Conversatie in de achttiende eeuw.* (Assen, 1968), pp. 175-78.

33. Abbé Perau, *L'Ordre des franc-maçons trahi, et le Secret des Mopses révélé,* Amsterdam, 1745, pp. 120-22; and J. L. Carr, "Gorgons, Gormogons, Medduists and Masons," *Modern Language Review*, LVIII, 1963, pp. 73-74. Cf. Harry Carr, ed., *The Early French Exposures*, London, 1971, p. 113 et seq., *La Franc-Maçonne ou révélation des mystères des francs-maçons par Madame****. Brussels (1744). In the Grand Lodge manuscripts two folios entitled "Tableau des Mopses" in an eighteenth century hand are all that remains of what may have been an interest in this organization.

34. *Livre de Constitution*, f.l. I am very grateful to Margaret Hunt for assistance with this text.

35. *Livre de Constitution*, f. 8. There were other, lesser offices in this lodge (as in most others), also given in both genders:

un frère inspecteur	*une soeur inspectrice*
Un frère M. des cérémonies	*une soeur maîtresse des cérémonies*
Un frère preparateur	*une soeur préparatrice*
un frère architecte	*une soeur architecte*

36. *Maconnerie d'Adoption Ecossoise*, 1751, ms in folder with *Livre de Constitution*, f. 11, ceremony entitled "Ouverture de la Loge." It begins with the instruction: "Les frères et soeurs entrent dans la chambre du travail et prennent chaucun leur place."

37. Ibid., ff. 15-16. Ceremony labelled "Reception au grade d'architecte" and f. 25-26, "Catéchisme des architects de l'adoptions écossoise."

38. *The Radical Enlightenment*, p. 253. The MS letter is housed at the University Library, Leiden, and is addressed to Prosper Marchand. The passage reads: "Nous sommes amis de tous le monde, excepté des Jesuites, dont aucun maître de loge ne voudrait recevoir un seul dans notre ordre . . .", in Marchand ms. 2, f. 36, item 8.

39. *Livre de Constitution*, f. 2, third paragraph, begins: "Conséquemment, nous freres et soeurs: Soussignés Declarons, et promettons, de Reconnoitre pour grand Maître des loges de maçonnerie d'adoption qui s'étableront dans les provinces unies." While f. 4 begins, "Au nom du grand architecte de l'univers avis à tous les frères et soeurs répandus sur la surface de la terre. Nous très haut et très puissant protecteur grand maître de toutes les loges des maçons et maçonnes établiées dans la souveraineté des provinces unies."

40. *Almanach des Francs-Maçons pour l'Année 1751*, (The Hague, Pour le Compte de la Fraternité, 1751), no pagination. A pocket size book of no more than 40 pages, the annual Masonic almanac is an invaluable source of information on the lodges in various countries. For other songs used in lodges of adoption see *Nouveau Recueil de Chansons de la Tres-Vénérable Confrairie des Franc-Maçons . . .* Berlin, n.d., pp. 65, 83-84, songs for women masons, possibly from the 1750's. The Grand Lodge of The Netherlands has one of the best collections of these almanacs in the world.

41. This copy of *Chansons de l'Ordre de l'Adoption . . .* Au temple de l'Union, Le premier May 1751, à la Haye, is at the Bibliothèque Nationale, Paris, YE 17876. I am extremely grateful to Professor Gordon Silber who discovered this tract.

42. Ibid, p. 4.

43. *Livre de Constitution*, f. 9: "Que tous frères et soeurs auront pour vêtement de maçons et de maçonnes, un tablier et des gants de peau blanches. Le tablier doublé de taffetas blanc et garni de ruban même couleur: qu'iles posteront pour simbolle de leur travail . . ."

44. J. Fransen, *Les comédiens français*, p. 304 (fl. is the symbol for a gilder). See also Franz Pick and Rene Sedillot, *All the Monies of the World—A Chronicle of Currency Values*, (New York, 1971).

45. Fransen, p. 305.

46. Richard W. Ungar, *Dutch Shipbuilding before 1800*, (Amsterdam, 1978), p. 91, Cf. Jan de Vries, "An Inquiry into the Behaviour of Wages in the Dutch Republic and the Southern Netherlands, 1580-1800" in *Acta historiae neerlandicae*, X, 1978, p. 96, where we learn that in Haarlem and Leiden in 1759 a stableman earned 312 fl. per annum while in Ghent in 1760 a servant earned 120 fl. p.a.

47. Fransen, p. 218.

48. The Library of the Grand Lodge, MS entitled "Mémoire Général de la Recette et de la Dépense des finances de la loge d'adoption depuis l'origine de la loge, jusques, et compris l'assemblée du onze d'avril". Only three months are included and the lodge met once almost every week in that period.

49. R. Ungar, *Dutch Shipbuilding*, p. 91. The fee was 63 fl.

APPENDIX

CATECHISM OF THE ARCHITECTS OF THE SCOTTISH RITE OF ADOPTION*

Le Vénérable: My sister, are you a masonic architect of the Scottish rite?

La Surveillante: Yes, most venerable one, the work is known to me.

Le V: How came you to this work?

La S: By traversing the quarries from north to east, and from south to west, [and crossing] the center.

Le V: In which location have you worked?

La S: The west.

Le V: What has your work produced?

---

*The Grand Lodge of the Netherlands, Ms entitled "Maçonnerie d'Adoption Ecossoise, 1751", ff. 25-29 are described as "Catéchisme des architectes de l'adoption écossoise." The translation from the original French seeks not to be literal, but to be usable by English readers.

La S:	A column.
Le V:	Out of which quarry was it mined?
La S:	The one in the center.
Le V:	Why?
La S:	Because the center is the first principal and the source of all things; without which no work can be completed.
Le V:	What purpose does this column serve?
La S:	It supports the edifice we are building.
Le V:	Which edifice is that?
La S:	The Temple of Virtue.
Le V:	This Temple, then, is being built without cement?
La S:	On the contrary, a cement of indescribable strength is employed there.
Le V:	Of what does this cement consist?
La S:	Quick-lime, sulfur, saltpetre, gunpowder and water.
Le V:	Is not this mixture dangerous?
La S:	No, venerable one; the union of all the parts reduces to a single substance sufficient to cement our columns.
Le V:	What is this single substance?
La S:	Fire.
Le V:	How does this transmutation take place?
La S:	By the process of aspersion.
Le V:	What do you mean by aspersion?
La S:	I mean the introduction of water into my cement compound.
Le V:	How is it possible for water, the enemy of fire, to ignite these combustible materials?
La S:	Freemasonry guards this mystery unto itself.
Le V:	What is the fruit of this mystery?
La S:	The knowledge of the name that I must henceforth carry in the order.
Le V:	What is this name?
La S:	It is the name of a virtue.
Le V:	Why the name of a virtue?
La S:	So that it can serve as an emblem on my column.
Le V:	Is this emblem sufficient for you to be recognized?

La S:	No, Venerable One, we also have five [secret] signs.
Le V:	What are those five signs?
La S:	Two gestures, a fulcrum, a touch and a word. [At this point in the ceremony the first four signs are called for.]
Le V:	Give me the word.
La S:	Nejusrimatea.
Le V:	What does that word signify?
La S:	Production.
Le V:	Through what means?
La S:	Through work.
Le V:	Where is your lodge situated?
La S:	In the quarries of Freemasonry.
Le V:	Where are they situated?
La S:	In the four extremities of the east, the west, the south and the north, with one in the center.
Le V:	What is found in the center?
La S:	The emblem of the order.
Le V:	What is the emblem of the order?
La S:	A living ermine which is the symbol of virtue.
Le V:	What illumines it?
La S:	The primitive light.
Le V:	What are the principle duties of masonry?
La S:	To listen, to obey, to work, to be industrious and to keep the secret.
Le V:	My brothers and sisters, since virtue is our emblem and since our quarries will always be places of delight as well as of industry, there comes a time when we conclude our labor and welcome the tranquility that follows it. Brothers and sisters the lodge of the architects of Scottish Masonry is now closed. Let us cease work and industry; let us listen and obey.

[The ceremony ends with *Le Vénérable* rapping five times with his mallet, and he is answered by *La Surveillante*. This gesture is then repeated by the assembled and all shout the word "Houzère", a term of unknown origin used to this day by freemasons of the Scottish rite as the rough equivalent of "Hurrah".]